ÉTIENNE GARBUGLI

The SaaS Email Marketing Playbook

Convert Leads, Increase Customer Retention, and Close More Recurring Revenue With Email

First edition

ISBN: 978-1-7780740-9-7

Editing by Joy Sellen

This book was professionally typeset on Reedsy.
Find out more at reedsy.com

To my mother, gone too soon.

Contents

III   Execution

IV   Optimization

V   Conclusion

VI Deep Dives

Acknowledgement

This book wouldn't have been possible without the instrumental contributions of past colleagues and managers at LANDR, Aeroplan, and beyond.

Early Reviews

"40–60% of your first-time users will check out your product and never come back. A good email marketing strategy is often the main difference between users coming back and never touching foot again in your product. This book shows you how to build a SaaS email marketing strategy that actually works." Wes Bush, Author, Product-Led Growth

"Etienne's book helped us set up all of our initial emails for our SaaS business—Pipeline. This book is very valuable to new SaaS businesses because it will show you how to get more subscribers from free trials, retain users, and even get back subscribers who cancel their subscriptions. I think anyone with a SaaS business will find something that can increase conversions from this book. Highly recommended!" Greg Davis, Founder & CEO, Pipeline

"I feel like I got an upgraded version of myself after going through the book. Etienne has in-depth knowledge of email marketing. The deep dives, cheatsheets, and case studies provided with this book were invaluable, and saved me tons of work. This book is a real must for SaaS founders and marketers." Saroj Ativitavas, Co-Founder & CEO, Wisible

"A well-written book for those who want to learn about SaaS email marketing from A to Z: how to create, segment and send successful campaigns, what templates to use, and how to optimize key elements. Etienne Garbugli has put together dozens of lessons, which are divided into logical and easily-digestible chapters. It's all very easy to read and extremely useful. I definitely recommend this book!" Jacek Krywult, CEO, PWSK

"The world would be a better place if B2B marketers stopped spamming and sent more well-targeted and well-crafted emails—and everyone would also sell more! Etienne Garbugli has put together a great no-BS resource where you are guaranteed to pick up useful tips and approaches, whether you're an email pro or just starting out." Andrus Purde, Founder & CEO, Outfunnel

I

Introduction

1

Why This Book?

Unless you're working for a large organization, your job title probably isn't 'email marketing specialist'.

Chances are that you have either volunteered, or you were selected as the most qualified person to handle email marketing.

Either way, you are accountable to make it work, and that can really be overwhelming. You may be thinking:

- *"How do you get started?"*
- *"How do you design effective emails when the design team is busy designing the product?"*
- *"How do you write effective copy when you're not a copywriter yourself (or don't have one on your team)?"*
- *"How do you get the right data and segments to make sure your emails reach the right users at the right time?"*
- *"How do you measure the return on investment of your campaigns?"*
- *"How do you avoid burning through your whole list?"*

And, most importantly: *"Wasn't email supposed to be dead?!"*

That's what I probably assumed when I got started at LANDR, a freemium SaaS platform in the music industry.

I turned to email a bit as a last resort. Too late...

Because it took months to get started, we probably lost a lot of users and revenue.

It turns out that it's really hard to reactivate and reengage users when you haven't been messaging them at all.

But that's also the beauty of SaaS email marketing. Improvements in conversions impact both current AND future users.

By making a single change today, you could significantly grow conversions.

In fact, if you do email marketing well, you can:

- increase product onboarding completion and engagement across the customer lifetime;
- increase trial-to-paid conversions and upgrade to paid plans;
- increase feature discovery and product engagement;
- reduce churn; and
- increase average revenue per user (ARPU), monthly recurring revenue (MRR), and the customer lifetime value (CLV).

You can get the benefits of those increases predictably, and repeatedly. You just need the right processes and knowledge.

Email marketing is one of the highest-leverage activities in a SaaS business.

I wrote this book to help product teams and SaaS marketers leverage email as a way to grow their business predictably.

In this book, you'll learn how to:

- create new emails to influence user behaviors and purchase decisions;
- create processes and structure to systematically grow the performance of your email marketing program;
- double, triple, or quadruple the performance of every single email you send; and
- avoid the countless mistakes I've made learning SaaS email marketing.

After reading this book, you'll be able to increase product onboarding completion, trial-to-paid conversion, and overall revenue with email.

When I joined LANDR, we were only sending three automated emails (and only one of them was working). By focusing on sending the right email to the right user at the right time performance jumped up with, among other things, an upsell program generating up to 42% of weekly subscription sales.

That's conversions we probably wouldn't have got without email.

This book will teach you everything I know about SaaS email marketing.

Once optimized, your lifecycle emails will deliver predictable growth and performance, literally printing money for your organization.

Let's take your business to the next level and add email marketing to your skillset.

Let's get this going.

2

Why Email Marketing Still Matters Today

Every year, email is declared dead.

Surely, social media, chat, voice, bots, or even augmented reality have killed it, *right?*

Yet each year email marketing keeps delivering a return on investment (ROI) as high as $42 for every dollar spent[1], much better than search and social media[2].

Why?

- Email is direct, it's personal.
- It's already part of everyone's habits.
- 99% of users check their emails daily[3].
- It's push, not pull.

In other words, if you have permission (which you should), your emails will usually *at least* get considered by your users.

This makes it one of the most effective channels at engaging, re-engaging, upselling, and retaining SaaS users.

No matter how great your product is, it's very likely that 40–60% of your free trial users won't see your product a second time[4].

This means that you stand to lose 60+% of your hard-earned signups. *Do you just let them go?*

Maybe you have access to their mobile numbers, or have their Facebook profiles. Perhaps you can send text messages or do retargeting, but these channels are more expensive and often less proven than email.

Email, to this day, remains the best channel to build relationships and bring users back into your product.

Done well, it has the potential to change minds and influence behaviors.

Email allows you to own the relationship. It can make your promos successful, amplify feature discovery, systematically grow conversions, and build habits.

In other words, it can help you maximize customer success while freeing you up to work on other high-leverage activities, like building a product.

You don't need to be a master copywriter (or have one on you team) to send effective emails.

In the next chapter, I'll show how to use emails to grow your business.

3

The Right Way to Think about Email and Marketing Automation

I got my start in email marketing in 2005. At the time, I was working for a retail chain in Canada called Bikini Village. We had created a Flash game that had gone viral. Thanks to the campaign, we had acquired over 300,000 email addresses.

And by that, I mean *only* email addresses.

While sometimes we had managed to capture the subscriber's first and last names, some preferences for brands, and (occasionally) the store of origin, usually the email address was *all* we had.

Soon thereafter, we began sending newsletters with the aim of nurturing and monetizing our 'database'.

But we were sending the same thing to all recipients regardless of:

- the context—where they signed up from;
- the timing—newer and older signups were handled the same way;
- past purchase behaviors and purchase intent—it didn't matter what

products subscribers were interested in;
- their preferences; or
- their behaviors.

All we were doing was a basic language split. We had one list for English speakers, and one for French.

This led to results that were *OK* for the time, but not amazing.

And that made complete sense to me.

Benefits were bland and generic, visuals weren't tailored to any specific segment, and messaging wasn't personal, or even relevant to most recipients.

But this was in 2005.

Sadly, these are the same mistakes that many marketers still make today.

A key reason for this is that marketers view an email or user list as a mere *list*. And this line of thinking leads to the idea that everyone is the same.

As a result, marketers end up sending the same messages to everyone—not thinking through each recipient's context—and using newsletters for engagement.

It's the only thing everyone will find relevant, *right?*

This leads to underperforming email campaigns, contacts that get burnt, and an overall under-appreciation of the value of email.

Mastering SaaS email marketing requires a change of mindset.

To be successful, you have to go from *list-thinking* to *database-thinking*

—understanding that contacts have different experiences and attributes.

They may differ in terms of their signup dates, their levels of engagement, languages, preferences, spend, subscription plans, goals, worldviews, etc.

Don't get me wrong! Every single person on your lists will still be worth contacting—they just won't be worth contacting for the same reasons.

Email marketing automation enables "personalized" communications at scale, so that you can:

- send the right message at the right time to the right people;
- go from list-thinking to a database and relationship marketing mindset;
- move away from one-off campaigns to workflows; and
- transition from "one-size-fits-all" to tailored and personal communications.

This change of mindset will help you grow performance across the customer journey and increase lifetime value. Most importantly for your users, it will improve their experience, and reduce the number of contacts and leads you burn.

SaaS is relational and data-driven by default—your email marketing should be as well!

The days of the "email blast" are long gone.

It's time to change your mindset and start thinking of each and every contact for what they are: people, like you and me.

This book will help you figure out how to serve them better.

4

How to Use This Book

At LANDR, we were sending 300 different emails, and were adding new language versions almost every month.

For Lean B2B, I have about 40 different emails sending.

For Highlights, the SaaS business I co-founded, I had about 30 emails and In-App messages sending at any given moment.

Chances are that, at this point, you're nowhere near as convinced as I am of the value of email marketing.

But if you have bought this book, it's probably because you have a hunch that email can be big for your business. And that's completely reasonable.

My response is: **let email prove its value to you, first**.

The content of this book was designed in layers:

- First, it has everything you need to create a basic email program. However, if you want to go further, there's enough content to take things very very far.

- In the Strategy section, we look at key SaaS milestones, core email sequences, and data segmentation strategies.
- The Execution section covers pacing, copywriting, and email analysis post-send.
- And sprinkled throughout the book are advanced tips for reporting, data management, optimization, team structure, and more.

This book *should* make you money. Lots of it!

It should allow you to predictably grow engagement, sales, and retention across your user base.

You can read it at your own pace—you don't need to optimize if you don't have the bandwidth to do proper email optimization.

Start with the basics, see how it feels, and let email prove its value to you. Advanced tactics will be there waiting when you're ready for them.

This book is meant to drive action and help you grow your business. If you don't intend to take things further, I will gladly refund the money you paid for it.

But if you do believe email can help, you'll see exactly where to get started in the next section.

Onwards!

II

Strategy

5

Email Marketing Doesn't Have to be Complicated

We have already talked about the importance of viewing your user list more as a database than a contact list. And we discussed how this means that each user has different attributes and needs to be handled differently.

So this means that you need to create hundreds and hundreds of emails, *right?*

Wrong.

When we started working on maximizing upsells across our entire user base at LANDR, there were users who had already been with us for two years.

We looked for patterns worth targeting across signup cohorts (groups of users defined by their common signup period) and segments. This allowed us to identify engaged users, churners, users with a lot of one-off product purchases, and so on. We were able to find literally dozens and dozens of patterns worth targeting. Then we used proven upsell messaging to test the waters.

As we began adding more and more emails and revenue grew, we started running into issues with email campaign overlaps. The same users received different offers and messages on the same day, or during the same week while some users received absolutely no emails from us.

Our support team was getting frustrated. We were struggling. As seasons changed, email volume fluctuated. The whole thing was a mess. It was clear that our program wasn't going to scale.

SaaS is *predictable*.

B2B, B2C, enterprise, SMB, users/businesses—the happy path in SaaS is pretty consistent:

1. People sign up, or you sign them up.
2. They get onboarded.
3. You try to convert them into customers.
4. They purchase, or not.
5. They engage, or not.
6. They churn, or not.

It's one of the reasons why Dave McClure's AARRR framework[5] (metrics for pirates) is such a great way to track the state of users.

Users are only in one *main* state at a time: Onboarding OR Paid subscriber OR Churned.

The issues we had ran into made us come up with what we ended up calling the "train track approach".

In the train track approach, each user is on the most appropriate train track based on his or her behavior. At each "station", we, the business, make an assessment of which communication program is best for their current behavior. When users change status, they go on a different track.

As an example, video analytics company Wistia has three tracks just for trial users:

- onboarding
- Aha moment achievement
- conversion

At LANDR, we had tracks for:

- onboarding
- paid subscribers
- onboarded, non-subscribers
- churners
- reengagement

All of these programs had clear start and end points, and their own unique objectives.

For onboarding, it was activation, the moment when users became active users of the product. For paying subscribers, it was retention. For churners, it was re-subscription.

The train track approach minimized overlaps and made sure no balls got dropped. It helped simplify user tracking across the customer journey, even as the business grew and scaled.

Your emails are meant to move the users along the awareness spectrum.

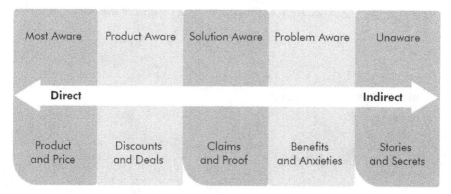

Figure 5.1 – Eugene Schwartz's "Five Levels of Awareness"

As copywriting expert Joanna Wiebe says: "It's not (supposed to be) a collection of random emails – it's a funnel."

You can decide to do things the hard way by adding individual emails in a pool of emails, excluding every single campaign from one another (please don't!), or you can create programs, and track users across those programs.

This book is about the latter approach.

In the upcoming chapters, we'll define the right tracks for your business based on your objectives.

6

The Key Milestones of SaaS, Explained Simply

Software as a Service businesses have surprisingly similar mechanics.

Users or customers sign up. They go through product value discovery. They are either convinced of the value of the product, or they're not. If they are, then they upgrade, are retained, and (hopefully) end up recommending the product. If they aren't, they cancel and they churn.

Now, whether your business is B2B or B2C, either you are the one creating their account or they are, either they pay before using, or after a trial, or they upgrade on their own terms with a freemium model. Those will be the key steps that you need to focus on.

What this means is that, there are really only a few milestones that matter:

1. **Signup**: the initial account creation
2. **Activation**: the Aha moment when the user perceives the product as valuable
3. **Conversion**: when a user agrees to swipe their credit card and purchase the product, or when a colleague does it for them

4. **Re-Purchase or Retention**: when users *willingly* pay for a second month, or a second year of subscription

5. **Referral**: when users refer your product to other prospects

Breaking down the SaaS customer experience into these milestones helps create clear start and end points for each track. It helps to understand that the next milestone after signup is activation, and that the first milestone for a paid subscriber is retention.

Milestones give you direction, a structure for assessing user states, and goals for next steps.

In the next chapter, we will look at key email sequences, and the main emails within each.

7

The 6 Email Sequences You'll Need (And the Key Emails within Them)

Signup, Activation, Conversion, Re-Purchase, and Referral.

We know the milestones, *now what?*

Your role as an email marketer—or someone trying to become one—is to help speed up transition from one milestone to the next.

Between each of these milestones will be successes (users who reach the next milestone) and failures (users who get stuck at an earlier stage). In spite of your best efforts, some users won't activate, some won't buy, and some will churn.

You need ways to handle both successful and unsuccessful users. And different sequences and stages require different tones, targetings, and goals.

Let's look at these different sequences and how to handle them specifically.

1. From Lead to Signup

First, *do you have access to emails prior to signup?*

Maybe you have a newsletter, blog signups, sales leads, or a pre-launch list you'd like to nurture to convince people to sign up for your product. If you do, the goal of your first sequence will be to convince these subscribers of the unique value of your product.

For this sequence, you have to balance the value of what the prospects actually signed up for (content updates for example) against pushiness.

The tone of this sequence will be more laid back. Key emails will be the welcome email for your series, and your ask to sign up.

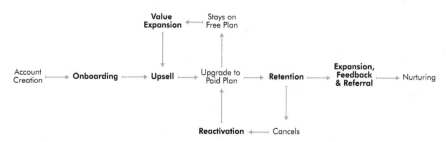

Figure 7.1 – The SaaS Lifecycle Email Program

2. From Signup to Activation (a.k.a. Onboarding)

For this phase, your goals are to help establish product value and to ensure users achieve their desired outcome with your product.

The tone should be informational and straight to the point.

These emails are about discovery, overcoming objections, and getting users back into your product.

Key emails will be your welcome email, and your first onboarding emails. Not only will these emails get opened more than any others (novelty), they will help you capitalize on the initial signup momentum (excitement).

Chances are that, if users delay in getting started, they won't ever get around to using the product.

You'll need to plan for users who don't activate. At LANDR for example, we were experimenting with communications based on the time that it took for users to activate— the velocity. This can be a good thing to look at when working on onboarding.

3. From Activation to Conversion (a.k.a. Upgrade)

The key email for this phase is the upgrade email. This one can be a bit pushy, or more *salesy* to drive conversions.

Here your goals are to confirm the product value, to remind the user how valuable the product is, and to capitalize on activation momentum if they did activate.

This sequence doesn't have to end at the upgrade. If your users don't convert and decide to stay on the free plan or give up on their trial, you can give them more reasons to upgrade with value expansion emails: 'Hey, our product also allows you to do X'.

It's always a good idea to eventually try to close them again, approaching it from a different angle. We will see how to do that in the Upgrade, Upsell & Expansion Revenue deep dive later on.

4. From Conversion to Retention

Your retention email sequence technically can last forever. Because of that, and because you are dealing with your VIPs, this often needs a different tone and a different strategy.

Although goals can vary depending on your business objectives (pure retention, expansion revenue, feature discovery, etc), the key objective is always retention and re-purchase. The best way to do this is to remind your users of the tremendous value that they are getting from your product.

You can do this with feature expansion, transactional emails, and launch emails which showcase more or different value in your product, or remind them of the value they are personally getting from the product with, for example, a summary email.

TextExpander does this very well. Each month, a summary email tells me how much time I saved thanks to their product:

Your Monthly TextExpander Report

Hi [First Name],

Payment Reminder:

This is just a friendly reminder that your annual billing is coming up in the next **30 days.**

Here's how you've been doing with TextExpander in the last month:

787
snippets expanded

1h 26m
saved

Doing well, keep it up!

Here are a few resources to give you some ideas for even more snippets. Check out our Public Groups for other ready-made snippet groups you can use.

We have lots of ideas for new snippets in our Tips center.

Check out our **Public Groups** for other ready-made snippet groups you can use.

TextExpander is chock full of neat features to help automate your typing floW, our **Videos** can tell you more.

We have lots of ideas for new snippets in our **Tips center.**

Figure 7.2 – TextExpander's Summary Email

5. From Retention to Expansion

Alternatively, you can also work on moving monthly subscribers to yearly subscriptions. This can be really effective when users are already engaged with your product. You can simply tell them how much money they will save by moving to an annual subscription, make a one-time offer, and watch the money roll in. You might not even need a discount to get upgrades.

This approach will both improve your cashflow, and reduce your churn rate.

Depending on your goal, you can also focus on expansion revenue: *Do you want to grow user seats? Feature usage?*

Look at consumption, and when an account is within 20% of maxing out a key value metric—what and how you're charging—send an email with an offer to upgrade their account to a more expensive plan. Experiment with discounting, and see how it goes.

This technique works great, and it's fairly easy to implement.

6. From Retention to Referral

You can have different asks for referrals from both paying subscribers and free users if your business has a freemium model.

Any referral email sequence will probably be sent out in parallel with other sequences.

To successfully get referrals, it's often a good idea to run Net Promoter Score (NPS) surveys, standardized surveys assessing how likely users are to recommend your product.

Based on scores 0 to 10, you can figure out which of your users are *Passives,*

Promoters, and *Detractors.*

Asking your Promoters (scores of 9 or 10) to help is a great way to get reviews or referrals, or to get them to invite more users.

Since you are working with your fans, the tone should be more casual and appreciative.

Key emails for this sequence will be your NPS Survey, and your specific ask. We will look at the referral sequence in depth in the Referral deep dive at the end of the book.

Sequence	Goal	Key Emails
Onboarding	Establish Product Value	Welcome + First Onboarding Email
Upsell	Confirm Value	Upgrade Email
Retention	Reinforce Product Value	Yearly Upsell + Transactional Emails
Reactivation	Build Back Product Value	Offer Upsell + Feedback Email
Value Expansion	Expand Product Value	Pivot Email + Upsell Email
Nurturing	Stay "Top of Mind"	Feature Launch Emails
Expansion	Increase ARPPU	Upsell Email
Referral	Gain Referrals	NPS Survey + Referral Emails
Feedback	Gather Insights	Survey or Interview Invite Emails

Figure 7.3 – Key Goals & Emails

Although you will probably want to expand and add other sequences down the road—reactivation, product feedback, etc—the sequences discussed so far are the fundamentals, the key foundations of your email program.

You can use the template at saasplaybook.co/traintracks to start defining and mapping your train tracks.

Start with these sequences and emails. Let the results prove themselves to you. Then expand your program from there.

8

Understanding Your Users and Customers

Let's take a step back.

How well do you know your users?

Are they of similar or different profiles?

What are they really trying to achieve with your product?

Even if you are targeting a very precise customer type, chances are that you are still dealing with quite different user roles and profiles.

Maybe these variations in profiles can be considered as 'marginal', or maybe they can't.

If you haven't already done so, I strongly recommend organizing series of interviews to understand your product's new signups.

To do so, look at signups from the past few months and create three buckets:

1. **Your best customers**: the top 1% in terms of engagement and revenue
2. **The next best**: customers ranked within the top 2–10%

3. **Your worst customers**: the bottom 10%

Depending on how technical you are, you may be able to find these users with SQL, a CRM, database exports, or by looking at people analytics in tools like Mixpanel, Amplitude or Intercom.

You want to focus on these three groups specifically because your top one percent represents your product's "fans", your advocates.

The next ten percent gives you a good comparison point. It can reveal low-hanging fruits that could help create an exceptional experience.

The bottom ten percent helps you define who you probably *shouldn't* be targeting, your anti-personas[6].

Reach out to users in each of these groups. Schedule 20-minute discussions, either over the phone, or face-to-face if it is possible.

You should do Switch interviews based on Jobs to be Done theory—the best interviews to understand the decisions leading up to using, or canceling a product.

These are great for signups, but also for purchases and cancellations.

You can find the interview template that I use at saasplaybook.co/interview.

You should ask questions like:

- *When did you purchase the product?*
- *Did anyone else weigh in on the decision?*
- *What was going on in your life when you first realized that this was a problem? How did you know?*
- *Where were you? What were you doing?*

- *What kind of solutions did you try? Or not try? Why? Or why not?*
- *How did you first hear about our product? What did you know about it at the time?*
- *Why did you decide to do something at all?*
- *Why did you sign up?*

Your core goal is to understand what people are trying to achieve with your product.

As you conduct these interviews, make sure you ask open-ended questions (*"Why?"* and *"How?"* not *"What?"* or *"Who?"*), avoid asking leading questions like *"Don't you think that this is a good idea?"*, and listen far more than you talk.

The ratio should be 90% listening, 10% talking. It's important to note that these are not discussions, they are interviews. Your goal is to learn, not talk.

Interview 10–20 users per segment, more if you find patterns you would like to dive deeper into. Once you are done, look at the data:

- *Were there noticeably different patterns?*
- *Were there opportunities to add value and improve product communications?*
- *Do you need to create deeper segmentation?*

Use these insights in conjunction with the analyses that you'll do over the course of the next few chapters.

Up next, we will take a closer look at your users and your segmentation strategy.

9

Understanding Segmentation Data

There's really no point in understanding your users, if you can't communicate with them specifically.

To be able to reach the right users at the right time, you will need segmentation.

There are four main ways to segment users:

1. By User or Buyer Persona

We talked about personas in the previous chapter. Unless you can turn user behavior data into recognizable personas (which is hard, but *not* impossible), you will need to find a way to categorize them into personas.

This can be done via self-identification through a survey, via manual assessments that review signups one at a time (this is time-consuming, often more realistic in large B2B), or by leveraging specific acquisition flows (for example tracking signups originating from a landing page targeting dentists specifically).

Those approaches could all help you understand persona data.

2. By Implicit Data

Implicit Data is information inferred from other available data. It can be seen as 'theories' about your users, or about your market in general.

For example, signups that originate from organic channels tend to have a higher purchase intent—and convert better.

This 'theory' could be used to inform communications and segmentation. Maybe you could push these users down your purchase funnel faster, or change the way you communicate with them specifically.

You often need to do a lot of experimentation in order to use implicit data as part of your segmentation strategy. Be mindful of the cost of doing so here.

3. By Explicit Data

Explicit Data is information captured through a form, a survey, or a setup process. People signing up – or giving you information – are aware that they are being asked questions and are knowingly giving you answers.

Biases and data input errors can break your segmentation, but sometimes this type of data will be the most valuable data you have.

There is always a balance to be struck between asking for more information (more fields tend to mean less completions), and getting people to sign up and act quickly.

It's especially important to be aware of the friction that you may be adding by capturing information before a user is actually convinced of the value of your product.

4. By Leveraging Behavioral Models

Behavioral segmentation leverages transaction and engagement data to create 'profiles'.

A popular framework for behavioral segmentation is the RFM framework.

RFM stands for:

- **Recency**: *How recently did the customer purchase?*
- **Frequency**: *How often do they purchase?*
- **Monetary**: *How much do they spend?*

Although RFM is more commonly used in e-commerce, it can still be effective in SaaS.

A frequent issue with behavioral targeting for email campaigns is that send volumes tend to vary depending on engagement and purchases. Because of this and seasonality, send volumes can vary significantly throughout the year.

With segmentation, less is more.

Simple segmentation helps prevent problems and also makes it easier to collaborate on campaigns, because everyone can understand the targeting the same way.

Clear patterns and targetings are also easier to write for and to assess. It will always be easier to write an email for dentists in Iowa, than for people with two plus sessions and a Gmail email address. Less projection is required in order to write email copy.

Although we had access to a ton of explicit, implicit, and behavioral data at

LANDR, we mostly relied on explicitly-stated personas for targeting.

There were clear issues with our persona data (which was based on roles), but it gave us the best balance between simplicity of data collection and accuracy of targeting.

Your segmentation criteria might be limited by your analytics setup or by the data that your email marketing platform can use.

With Highlights, we were sending key product events to Intercom, our email marketing platform for behavioral targeting. This allowed us to send different personal follow-up emails based on early usage and setup.

Understanding segmentation is critical. It's what allows you to reach the right users at the right time, create a better customer experience, and reduce the risk of overwhelming your users.

In the next few chapters, we'll look at the types of data that you need to send to your email marketing platform in order to make your segmentation work.

10

Mapping Customer Journeys

A common mistake made by businesses is to think of email marketing in isolation: as something quite distinct from all the other interactions they have with their prospects, users, and customers.

In reality marketing emails are rarely the only 'emails' that users and prospects receive from these businesses, and in the eyes of users, all emails add up.

For this reason, it is important to consider the totality of end user communications when assessing the current situation.

This might mean:

- **Transactional emails**: For various reasons (cost, the need to use variable content, or the ease of implementation for developers), many businesses will use both a transactional and a marketing email platform. This can often result in a disjointed experience for users.
- **Transaction receipts**: *Do your payment gateways or accounting solutions contact users on your behalf? It's important to find out!*
- **Issue trackers, customer support, and customer success platforms**: *Do your CS platforms send emails for follow-up or feedback? Do your CRM or*

sales staff contact or re-contact users on your behalf? Does the content team send newsletters? Can there be overlaps with those recipients? Are there other legacy or supporting systems contacting users?

Go through your entire business. Make sure you have a clear understanding of *all* the ways users and prospects get contacted by your organization.

Unless you replace them, anything you add will be *on top of* the communications already in place.

Try to get a clear picture of the customer journeys: all the way from first-thought (awareness) to signup, and beyond. The customer experience doesn't start at signup. It starts when prospects are first exposed to your brand, be it through ads, search results, or product reviews.

Identify your top five acquisition channels. This can be done from Google Analytics under Acquisition and Default Channel Grouping, or via the Source/Medium reports.

Review how your users experience your service, from their original channel interaction to the landing page to the signup and onboarding processes, and then your communications. The more scattered your program is, the harder it will be to piece the experience back together.

You may already be spamming your users without even realizing it (sadly, this often happens).

Try to understand any gaps in expectations and any inconsistencies. The more inconsistent the story you tell, the leakier your funnel will be. You need to tell the same story from start to finish. This helps to amplify the story and build up your business goals. Anything that tells a different story will create doubts in your users' minds.

Switch interviews can be done with users that have signed up from your top five channels, with the aim of getting their different takes on the experience (if this isn't done already).

You can ask:

- *Did it feel scattered?*
- *What helped?*
- *What hurt?*

Map the entire process. If there are things that don't move the needle, or that feel out of place, remove them.

Product-Led Growth author Wes Bush recommends printing out each step and every action that users need to take in your product, and asking:

1. *What steps can be eliminated?*
2. *What steps can be delayed?*
3. *What steps are mission-critical?*

All communications, from receipts to support follow-ups, *should* help drive performance. It's really important to evaluate everything in the context of your goals.

Once you are starting to get a clear picture of the *current* situation, move on to defining the future.

11

Defining Necessary Custom Fields

At this stage, businesses often tend to overthink their email data model.

This can lead to the creation of a complex solution that takes time to ship. Once that solution is implemented, it's hard to test and spot the issues. It is also difficult to onboard internal users, getting them to adopt it.

With some platforms—Intercom for one[7]—the number of custom fields is limited. An over-complex solution can ultimately limit opportunities later on.

Although none of these issues are deal-breakers, needs do change quickly in technology. It's almost impossible to know up-front what you will need in terms of data next year, let alone three years from now.

For this reason, it's best to keep things simple.

You may be tempted to add things—especially if it's hard to get engineering time in your organization—but you most likely won't need *everything*.

Here is an acceptable Minimum Viable Analytics Product (MVAP) for many SaaS businesses:

1. **Profile basics**: These include first name (for personalization), email address, user type, subscription status, signup date (many platforms will add this; if yours doesn't, then add it), language, sessions, country, and time since last visit.

2. **Status information**: You need a way to evaluate where the user is within your program (trial, paid subscriber, churned, re-paying). This can be done by combining custom fields. For example, a status and a signup date, or with a dedicated field. Either approach can work.

3. **Revenue metrics**: Ideally, revenue information should come directly from the database for accuracy reasons. Revenue metrics can be used to calculate user value or subscription types.

4. **Value metric**: A value metric is what you use to evaluate how much value your users are extracting from your product. Your value metric will often be tied to your activation rate, your pricing model, and the way you evaluate user engagement. If you don't currently have a value metric, then dissect your pricing model—*what key elements can help with segmentation?* Use those. For example, at LANDR it was the number of masterings, while for Highlights, it is the number of client accounts.

5. **(Optional) Specific goal metrics:** If you are focusing on a certain email sequence with its own unique goal, you can also decide to add a key goal metric. For example, the number of referral invites, or the number of successful referrals if you're trying to increase referrals. These types of calculated metrics can be your guiding light when running campaigns.

Keep things simple and expect change.

If you have clearly defined personas or segmentation, it can be a good idea to add those as well.

Other than these six or seven custom fields, I don't suggest adding much more when you are first starting out.

Although your email marketing automation platform can probably also be used for data analysis and user tracking, the data obtained won't be as reliable as data you can get from your analytics platform or database. For this reason, don't try to use your email marketing automation platform as your business's "source of truth".

Don't try to get too sophisticated too quickly. Start with the Minimum Viable Product (MVP). In the next chapter, we will look at implementation.

12

Creating a Data Implementation Plan

In the same way that the fields that you use will change and evolve over time, your implementation is also likely to change and evolve over time.

There are typically three distinct phases of analytics:

1. **The "Good Enough" phase**: In this phase, you don't have enough data to make decisions based on analytics. There may or may not be someone actively looking at the data, but because implementing analytics often competes with other core activities—like shipping a product—analytics are generally in a "set and forget" mode.
2. **The "Head Above Water" phase**: Once you're able to get your head above water and understand your business metrics a bit more clearly, investing in analytics starts to make a lot of sense. Because the business challenges are clearer, it becomes easier to find the right analytics product for the job. During this phase, it's often more important for the data to point in the right direction than for it to be entirely accurate.
3. **The "Accuracy" phase**: Because of outside pressures (often investors), or the desire to scale customer acquisition with reliable data, analytics eventually have to become 100% accurate. To reach this level of sophistication, businesses often invest in robust backend analytics or their own data warehouse. The analytics platforms might be the same,

but business intelligence platforms are often introduced to help query the data.

You should be able to tell which phase your business currently is in.

Your technical solution will most likely need to evolve along with your business. For this reason, it's often a good idea to start with a data management platform like Segment (Paid)[8], or Google Tag Manager (Free)[9].

These platforms act as layers between your app and the email and analytics products you use. This can allow you to change email and analytics platforms with relative ease, and sometimes even replay past data.

As you get started, sit down with product management, data, and/or engineering. Agree on the source of truth—the most reliable source—for each and every metric you'll need.

Discuss how the customer data will be synced (both ways ideally), the quality assurance (QA) process, how data will be sent, from where it will come (database, frontend, other), and how it will be replayed if the service is down or unavailable.

You want to have clear agreements as to what data you are supposed to use and the ways that data can be used. Grey zones are your enemy here.

For each field you want in the email marketing platform, make a list of:

- the source of truth;
- the type of data expected (for example dollar amount, boolean, Yes/No, a calculated metric, a count, or a status—Don't forget to list all the possible statuses for these fields);
- the label of the attribute or field used in the email platform.

To get started fast, you can use the template at saasplaybook.co/datafields.

Run each field by your colleagues. You want all labels to be clear and unambiguous. This will help reduce the number of questions everyone gets and increase personal ownership.

Share your plan with the product, data and engineering teams, gather questions, refine, adjust, and then monitor implementation.

Once your email marketing platform is starting to receive data in *Dev* or in *Prod*, move on to the next chapter for testing.

13

Creating Key User Segments

The beauty with segmentation is that it can be used for more than email targeting.

You can use your segmentation for tracking and reporting, to recruit candidates for interviews, and for quality assurance.

If your segmentation doesn't get you the *right* users, you want to find out as quickly as possible.

Before starting to write emails, you'll want to create key user segments.

Those could be:

- people who haven't signed up for your product (if the required data is available);
- people who signed up today;
- people who signed up in the last seven days;
- people who signed up in the last seven days, but didn't engage, or didn't activate;
- people who signed up in the last 30, 60 or 90 days and activated;
- inactive users;

- users whose trial is about to end or just ended and that you would eventually like to convert;
- paid subscribers in their first month;
- paid subscribers retained for two months or more;
- subscribers on annual plans;
- users who you think would be willing to refer your product to others;
- subscribers who cancelled;
- subscribers who cancelled more than once; or
- signups per specific acquisition channel.

Don't go too far, but do try to test real segments with real data. Let them run a few weeks. *Do users flow through the way you'd expect them to?*

Go through random profiles in each of these segments and compare with the data from your database. *Are those the users you'd expect to find in each of these segments? Any issues?*

You want to uncover issues with the implementation or your segmentation as early as possible. It's easier if you do this—and much less costly in terms of mistakes—*before* you start sending emails than after.

Make sure you can track users across different segments and that your segments truly are mutually exclusive when they need to be.

Identify issues, adjust, and refine. This step will save your team a lot of headaches later on.

As you test your segments, make them available to the rest of your team. Your colleagues can also help point out issues.

At this point, if there aren't any major issues, your setup is complete.

Let's get started sending some emails!

14

Creating Operating Rules for Your Program

You might be able to get away without rules and processes when you are getting set up with your email program, but as more people start to get involved, you'll have to set some basic rules and processes to allow your program to scale.

It's always better to be the one setting the rules, than to have them defined for you.

The rules that you will want to define will vary depending on who *owns* email marketing, and the responsibilities of each teams within the organization.

Email usually impacts:

- **Product/Product Marketing**: *How do you talk about the product? Which features get promoted? Which features don't get promoted? Where do you send the traffic? How does email work with the in-product onboarding?*
- **Brand & Marketing**: *Who writes the copy? What's the tone? How are news, promos, and feature launches handled? What are the processes for collaborating?*
- **Finances & Analytics**: *How do results get reported? How do you track ROI? What constitutes emails in terms of attribution? How is the data validated*

and audited?

- **Design**: *Who handles email design? What's the process for implementing new designs? What's the plan to sync up email designs with the rest of the brand and design assets when they change?*
- **Support & Customer Success**: *How are email responses handled? What happens when support has questions about email offers or any other communications? How are sales requests handled? How do tones and explanations get synced up?*
- **Management**: *Who owns email? What are the objectives or the KPIs? What kind(s) of approval(s) do you need before you press send? How do you get more budget or resources? What's the overhead?*

Email is customer-facing communications. As email starts to perform, it's very likely that it will attract other business stakeholders within the organization (politics!). You might not think that you will need rules and processes, but I strongly recommend you start answering the questions listed above.

Sit down with the product, brand, marketing, analytics, finances, design, and support leaders. Get alignment and share back the rules for email marketing within the organization.

You can use the template at saasplaybook.co/rules to get started fast.

You'll avoid a lot of problems by setting the basic rules of engagement before you go too far.

III

Execution

15

Unfortunately, It Won't Be Perfect

When we started working on email marketing at LANDR, I created a huge spreadsheet. It listed every campaign I thought we'd ever need: drip sequences, success messages, newsletters, Hail Marys, everything. It was based on the engagement metrics we had, and was mapped for months and months.

The goal was to get the team to buy in and use this "map" to prioritize email development.

At this point, we were speaking with users, analyzing tons of data, and had reviewed all support communications.

We had a strong hunch that a certain kind of email onboarding messages (based on use cases) would perform. So we wrote copy, had it reviewed, sent the emails to design, got completely new templates made, implemented them with front-end developers, and soon enough, we were ready to send our new email sequence.

The copy was clever and the emails were beautiful.

However, these emails didn't even manage to beat the existing emails, the ones that hadn't been performing originally...

Worse, these emails weren't even worth optimizing. They were just too far from the baseline.

Weeks of work down the drain.

At this rate, it would take years to get an email program to perform.

So, we axed design. We axed the clever copy. It was clear that no amount of upfront work would *guarantee* success.

We drastically reduced the time it took to implement emails. It went from weeks to hours. It wasn't uncommon for us to set three to four new emails live each week.

We used default templates, proven copy, and simple call-to-actions (CTAs). If the email worked, we would scale it and improve the layout, design, and copy. If it didn't, we would just kill it. No harm, no foul.

It was fast and efficient, but it also meant that we were sending a lot of imperfect emails.

It's easy to get caught up in the specifics of your emails and turn email creation into *Projects*, with a capital 'P'. The reality is though that details won't matter if people don't care about your offer.

There *will* be a time to polish your emails and improve the branding elements within them, but when you're first setting things up you want a quick feedback loop. There's a lot of ground to cover, and you won't have certainty on anything before you put it out there and test.

So, embrace imperfection. Failure is the cost of creating something great.

Focus on learning the answers to these questions first:

- *Is this the right email?*
- *Are we sending it to the right people?*
- *Does the timing work?*
- *Can the copy be improved?*

You'll have a clearer path to improving your emails once you start getting some results, and you will build certainty through experimentation.

Embrace imperfection first. Trust me, your emails *will* get better over time.

16

Prioritizing Your Email Roadmap

Chances are you'll need a Hail Mary. And a Net Promoter Score survey email. And a newsletter. And... And... And...

If you are getting started with your email program, the list of emails you'll need will probably be very long.

Do you need to do everything at once?

Definitely not.

In fact, it's best to start your program by aligning with business priorities and getting results before thinking about expanding.

What areas are most troublesome in your business right now? What metric are you expected to move with email? Is it:

- *Engagement?*
- *Retention?*
- *Conversion?*
- *Revenue?*
- *Signups?*

If none of those stick out above the rest, start from the top.

Welcome and onboarding emails set the tone for product usage. Better onboarding and value communication lead to reductions in churn and disengagement down the road. Welcome and onboarding emails are also sent to most, if not all, of your users, thus they have a greater potential to influence user behaviors.

At Highlights, for example, we set up a welcome email, five onboarding emails, and an upsell email the week before we launched the product.

The goal was to maximize the number of people in a position to convert. It also allowed us to start getting some data to optimize performance.

In general, you'll want to prioritize emails that:

1. send a lot (large volume of sends);
2. send consistently (every day, or every week at least); and
3. have the potential to have a big impact on a key business goal.

In the beginning especially, you want to make sure that you have a clear goal or metric to monitor with the aim of evaluating performance with user data.

Start implementing a first sequence, test, gather data, and move on to the next sequence.

17

Why Speed Matters

To get started testing and implementing emails you'll need, at a minimum, segmentation data (you don't want to send to everyone), email templates loaded up in your email marketing tool, and email copy.

Depending on your skillset and the resources at your disposal, this can be as easy as creating a small team with a dedicated analyst, a front-end developer, and a copywriter writing new copy for all your emails. But until email marketing proves itself to you, you probably want to stay lean as long as possible.

To get started fast, use:

- very simple segments (e.g. the number of days since signup);
- built-in templates with little to no customization or templates bought on ThemeForest[10] or similar sites (these templates will help make sure that your emails display well across email clients, devices, and operating systems); and
- email copy from other organizations to test copy ideas.

This is the other extreme. It might be *leaner* than what you're willing to do, but it can help you get started in under an hour.

The sooner you start sending emails, the sooner you start learning about what works and what doesn't.

As you build more comfort in your email program and learn from your audience, you'll be able to create more precise segments and improve your copy.

Don't get caught up in the specifics if you are just getting started. Barebone emails often outperform overly-engineered emails. Create velocity and start learning, first.

In the next chapter we'll look at different ways to source email inspiration.

18

Researching Email Copy & Designs

Here's the trick to significantly improving your SaaS email marketing skills—you have to become a student of it. This means you should:

- Start collecting great email copy, CTAs, and designs.
- Understand the objective behind each and every email that businesses send.
- Try to understand the rationale behind copy, link, and design decisions.

There are great websites like Really Good Emails[11], Good Email Copy[12], and Good Sales Emails.com[13] that you can use for your research. These sites categorize email copy and designs by types.

As well as this, you should sign up to receive emails from some of the leading SaaS brands. Those include, among others:

- Drift
- MailChimp
- Pipedrive
- Shopify
- SurveyMonkey
- Trello

- Wistia
- Zapier

You should also sign up to competing products and mailing lists from companies in your sector.

I personally signed up to thousands of products and newsletters. It's great for benchmarking and research. At the time of writing, I've already passively collected more than 60,000 emails.

Obviously, don't sign up to your competitors' products with a business email address!

I have a special email address I use for this. This account allows me to get data, understand what other organizations are doing, and find good copy ideas.

For example, here's what a search for 'Typeform' gives me:

Typeform 4	SendGrid	[Final reminder] Changes to your Typeform plan - It's happening tomorrow. Here's how this affects you ...	
Typeform 3	SendGrid	[Reminder] Changes to your Typeform plan - It's happening next week. Here's how this affects you and ...	
Typeform	SendGrid	[Reminder] Changes to your Typeform plan - It's happening next week. Here's how this affects you and ...	
Typeform 4	SendGrid	Changes to your Typeform account - Plus a coupon to ease the transition. Hello, I'm Kim, CEO of Typef...	
Typeform 4	SendGrid	Pricing changes that affect your account - Plus a coupon to ease the transition. Hello, I'm Kim, CEO of ...	
Robert from Typeform 2	autopilothq	SendGrid	Lend us your brain, win an iPhone XR - Hi, We're trying to figure out the best way to price Ty...
Typeform	autopilothq	SendGrid	We updated our terms. Cue gasps of excitement. - Hi there, We've updated our terms and C...
Typeform	autopilothq	SendGrid	We updated our terms. Cue gasps of excitement. - Hi there, We've updated our terms and C...
Typeform	autopilothq	SendGrid	We updated our terms. Cue gasps of excitement. - Hi there, We've updated our terms and C...
Typeform	autopilothq	SendGrid	We updated our terms. Cue gasps of excitement. - Hi there, We've updated our terms and C...
hello 2	SendGrid	Activate your Typeform account - Hello, you're a click away from accessing your Typeform account...	

Figure 18.1 – Inbox Inspiration

It's not uncommon for me to sign up several times to the same product or newsletter. This allows me to see what they have learned and to track the evolution of their email marketing program.

At LANDR, we created a shared document to keep track of subject lines, offers, and copy we wanted to test. Our copywriter was even going through his junk mail folder to find ideas and inspiration. There are tests we ran that were inspired by copy found in his spam folder. Some of them turned out to be really successful too—so keep your eyes open for inspiration. You can use Evernote, Paper, or any other platform to collaborate on idea generation.

Alternatively, you can subscribe to paid services like Mailcharts[14] or Mailody[15]. These services will help you track and understand your competitors' email programs.

Build processes to find and access copy and design ideas. It will help you create better emails, faster.

In the next chapter we'll get started creating our first email sequences.

19

Email Sequence Pacing & Structure

Ideally with emails, you'd like to send the absolute fewest number of emails, and achieve the maximum results.

One issue that you will face is that, until you start testing, email pacing will be more art than science.

There are times when sending emails three to four days apart will give great results. But there are also times when sending an email every day will give you optimal results.

As an example, social media scheduling platform MeetEdgar conducted an experiment with the pace of their onboarding email sequence[16].

What they realized was that they could get the exact same conversion numbers by cutting down their sequence from 30 to ten days. This meant that they could activate users much faster, with very few or no downsides. It also meant faster revenue growth and engagement. *What's not to love about it?*

To structure your email sequences, start with the end goal. *Is it conversion? Activation? Referral? Reengagement?*

The sequence you're working on should only have **one** main goal. This will help create focus.

As users achieve the goals, you'll want to move them to different sequences—the different train tracks that we talked about. This will improve the experience for your users and customers, and drive focused performance on your goals.

With this approach, sequences don't actually need to end. MailChimp, for example, sends about 12 onboarding emails, and they could certainly add more.

As long as your emails *add* to your sequences in both performance and usefulness, you can keep going until your users either activate, or they become completely disengaged.

Start from the top with your strongest arguments. Put a first email in place. Then evaluate performance, add a second email, evaluate the added impact—and keep going!

The key idea is that any email should add to the overall performance of your sequence. Every email that your users open but don't care about reduces the chance that they will open your future emails.

Although you can look at cohort retention curves and target engagement drop-offs to time your emails (what we did at LANDR), you'll probably get similar results by sending emails every other day, and experimenting with pacing once your sequence is in place.

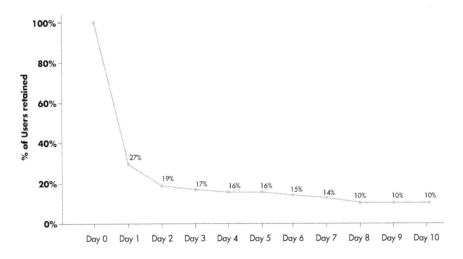

Figure 19.1 – Retention Curve Example

A two-day pace will only work for onboarding or nurturing emails. For other sequences (Upsell, Referral, or Feedback), start by rolling out a first email, evaluating performance, and then add follow-up emails or reminders 2–3 days after the original email.

Create your sequences with the goal in mind. Add emails one after the other. Use a default pace before experimenting with pacing.

Get started with this. We will push pacing further in Optimization later on.

20

Effective Email Copywriting

I'm not a copywriter. But I can write emails that sell, convert, and get people to act.

If I can do it, you can do it too. All you need is practice and the right guidelines. Here they are!

There are two distinct types of copy:

1. **Indirect response**: Copy that *eventually* leads to a sale over time by building trust and awareness. This type of copy tends to be best-suited to nurturing and branding emails.
2. **Direct response**: Copy that pushes for a purchase or an action *immediately* at the end of the copy. These emails are easier to test since their goal is to drive direct behavior.

Both types of copy have their uses. However for SaaS, because we're trying to get users to perform key actions, we'll mostly focus on the latter.

For direct response emails, your offer must flow from the subject line on down. Your email needs to tell a coherent story, and build momentum from the subject line to the preview text, all the way to the CTA.

You have to *demonstrate* how the readers will benefit. Don't talk about features or your company. Try to use more "you" than "I" or "we" to make your copy more relevant to your user's life.

The offer has to be logical and a clear follow-up to the copy; it shouldn't come out of nowhere. It has to be a deal that can't be refused. This can be done by removing options.

I like to use the nod test for this. You want users to nod in agreement as they read your email:

- "Yeah..."
- "Yeah... that's me"
- "Oh yeah..."
- "Of course I'll buy!"

Below are a few emails which I believe do this very well. You'll see what I mean. Casually read through the copy, and notice whenever you find yourself nodding along.

Drift – Feature Launch Email

Drift is a company building conversational marketing software out of Boston.

Soon after I signed up to use their platform, I received the following launch email:

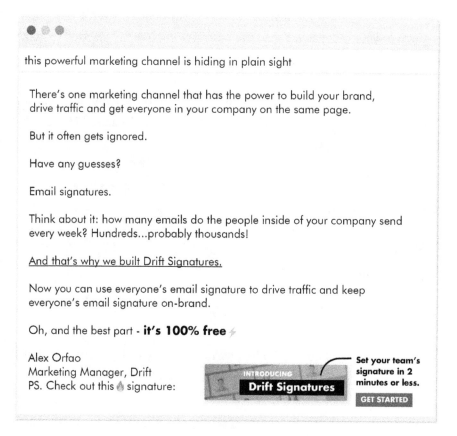

this powerful marketing channel is hiding in plain sight

There's one marketing channel that has the power to build your brand, drive traffic and get everyone in your company on the same page.

But it often gets ignored.

Have any guesses?

Email signatures.

Think about it: how many emails do the people inside of your company send every week? Hundreds...probably thousands!

And that's why we built Drift Signatures.

Now you can use everyone's email signature to drive traffic and keep everyone's email signature on-brand.

Oh, and the best part - **it's 100% free**

Alex Orfao
Marketing Manager, Drift
PS. Check out this signature:

INTRODUCING
Drift Signatures

Set your team's signature in 2 minutes or less.
GET STARTED

Figure 20.1 – Drift's Feature Launch Email

- The email's subject line ("this powerful marketing channel is hiding in plain sight") leverages curiosity to get users to open.
- It uses plain text and appears to be sent by an employee to make the email feel more personal.
- Each sentence flows from the previous, using curiosity again to get users to keep reading.
- The email clearly establishes the benefits before explaining what feature is being launched.
- Instead of explaining what the feature is, it uses the feature itself to

illustrate the benefit.

Zapier – Upgrade Email

Zapier helps automate API integrations.

A day before the end of my 14-day trial, I received the following email:

● ● ●

Your Trial Ends Tomorrow

Hey [First Name], Wade here,

Your free 14-day trial of Zapier's premium services ends tomorrow
(Oct 24, 2019 at 6:31 p.m. CST). That means you'll no longer have access to
Zaps with multiple steps, Premium Apps (like Salesforce, Zendesk, PayPal, and
others), or other paid features.

Once your trial ends, though, you'll be switched to the Zapier Free Plan.
It comes with 5 Zaps, 100 monthly Tasks, and updates every 15 minutes.

Any workflows you have that don't meet your plan's limits will be turned off.
But if you want to build automations with multiple steps or use other premium
features, you can upgrade to a Premium Plan.

Learn More About Premium Plans

Thanks for trying Zapier!

Wade Foster
Co-Founder & CEO of Zapier

P.S. If you didn't get enough time to try Zapier over the past two weeks,
simply reply to this email to let me know and we can extend your trial.

Figure 20.2 – Zapier's Upgrade *Email*

- The email is in plain text, sent from the company's CEO, which makes it stand out from the image-heavy onboarding emails I had received.
- Both the subject line ("Your Trial Ends Tomorrow") and the email's introduction establish that my free trial is about to end. The timing, one day before the trial ends, helps create urgency.
- The email makes it really clear which features I stand to lose. If I'm getting value out of the automations, I now know what I need to do.
- They offer a simple link to help me evaluate different subscription options.
- The email uses a P.S.—one of the most read parts in emails—to offer an alternative. This suggests I can keep using Zapier even if I don't upgrade.

Podia - Upsell Email

Podia helps creators sell online courses, digital products, and memberships.

As a subscriber on the monthly plan, I received the following email:

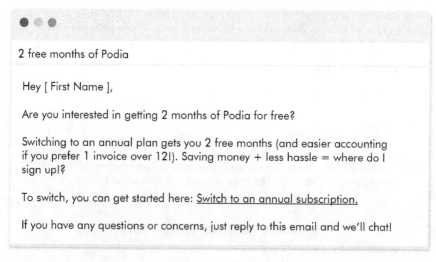

Figure 20.3 – Podia's Upsell Email

- The email's subject line ("2 free months of Podia") uses curiosity to get subscribers to open.
- The email quickly explains how I can save money, and what the benefits are.
- It's very easy to take action. The email has a clear CTA that links directly to the annual subscription flow for upgrades.
- The company CEO opens the door to questions to help overcome any hesitations.
- Overall, this is a very simple email that drives action. These types of emails tend to print money.

The following tools will help make your email copy *nod-worthy*:

1. Create intimacy:

You'll get more trust—and capture the attention of your prospects—by establishing a personal connection. Your emails should read as if one person has written it to another: one to one.

This can be achieved by:

- using a personal, or plain-text template;
- using "you" instead of "we", or "I";
- telling stories; and
- making good use of personalization.

For an even greater effect, you can add subtle personalization throughout your copy. For example: "…this is what we've heard from other people in [Tampa]".

2. Make users feel special:

On top of personalization, you can create exclusivity:

- "This offer is only for *our most engaged users*"
- "...it's for *early adopters*"

Or appeal to vanity:

- "Our most *successful* users want to feel this way..."

3. Demonstrate that you understand their reality:

You can create obvious qualifications everyone wants to have assigned to themselves, for example "...people who care about maximizing their return on investment"; or "...savvy marketers".

Illustrate product benefits and value with clear examples that relate to the unique situation of your users.

4. Create urgency:

As Zapier did, you can also get creative with deadlines. Use coupons with limited-time offers to accentuate the fear of missing out (FOMO)[17]:

- "Offer only available until June 4th..."
- "Only a few people get this plan..."

5. Use clear actions:

- Use a CTA that clearly establishes the next steps. Repeat it throughout the email, coming at it from different angles.
- Use the P.S. to attract the eye and to reinforce the action you want users

to take (when appropriate).

- Keep your emails simple and your messaging scannable. It's important for users to be able to *get* the email at a glance.
- Short and sweet often outperforms long and complex emails. You want a near-instant reaction from your readers.

Your email has to build up to the desired action. Use copy to overcome objections, and accentuate the desire to buy or engage.

A good email has to:

1. *capture attention* through the subject line, personalization, or a story;
2. *build reader interest* by demonstrating either the benefit or the problem;
3. *build desire to act* by creating information gaps, time constraints, or the fear of missing out; and
4. *drive action* through a well-timed CTA, telling users exactly what you want them to do.

These are really just the four steps of the AIDA model[18] (Attention, Interest, Desire, and Action) applied to email copywriting.

Don't get intimidated by copywriting. Emails that are too polished often don't work as well. Get started crafting your own email offers. We'll get started working on subject lines in the next chapter.

21

Subject Line Copywriting

A lot has been said about the importance of subject lines in email marketing.

Subject lines have this aura of *mystique*. There's this idea that a great subject line can single-handedly make your campaigns successful.

But in reality, open rates are influenced by a combination of factors.

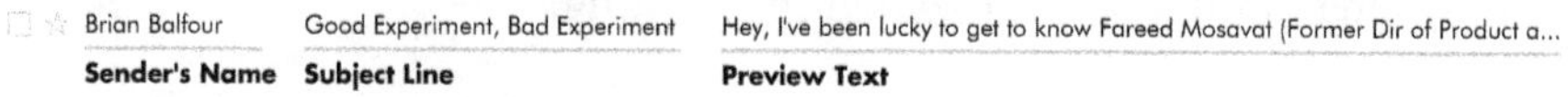

Brian Balfour	Good Experiment, Bad Experiment	Hey, I've been lucky to get to know Fareed Mosavat (Former Dir of Product a...
Sender's Name	**Subject Line**	**Preview Text**

Figure 21.1 – Open Rate Components

The subject line, the preview text, the sender's name, the sender's email address, whether the email fell in the inbox or the promotion tab, your brand, the trust you've built over time, the number of emails you send/have sent, the timing, and the competition for your user's inbox that day all factor into that user's decision to open (or not) your email.

When it comes to subject lines, you want to evaluate:

- **Scannability**: *Does it catch the eye?* Numbers, personalization, and emojis tend to stand out in the inbox;

- **Concision**: Subject lines of 55 characters or less are generally ideal. Think about both the length of the words you use, and the length of the entire subject line;
- **Reading level**: The lower the reading level, the better. It's generally a good idea to aim for grades 5 or 6;
- **Sentiment**: Positive sentiment tends to perform better across campaigns;
- **Spam trigger words**: Spam words tend to change over time. It's a good idea to stay current on the various lists[19]. Generally, you want to avoid words like « free », « re: » (reply), « fwd: », and exclamation points;
- **Tabulation**: Bad tabulation and ALL CAPS subject lines feel promotional. Title Case, or even all lowercase subject lines usually perform better.

It's important to be able to capture your audience's attention.

As we have seen, good subject lines can trigger curiosity with mystery. This can be done by asking questions, or using cliffhangers. For example:

- "You've earned it." (Opened at 69%);
- "Boom! You Just Went Gold!" (Opened at 62%, in spite of the exclamation marks);
- "Is it time to upgrade your workflow?" (Opened at 56%).

They can also create a sense of urgency. If you are running a promo, you can create scarcity by hinting at the fact that there's only a limited quantity, or a limited number of days left.

- "Last day for your early adopter discount" (Opened at 51%);
- "VIP Subscription Offer" (Opened at 40%);
- "Last Chance For Your VIP Subscription" (Opened at 31%).

They can also be personal or contextual:

- "Hey [John], I came up with something for you" (Opened at 55%);
- "[John], How do other composers and songwriters land your contracts?" (Opened at 53%);
- "Why leave? The party just started" (Opened at 48%).

They are concrete, or tied to specific actions the user has taken, or is trying to take:

- "You're Eligible for a Privileged Account" (Opened at 62%);
- "Can I help?" (Opened at 60%);
- "Thanks for Signing Up to Our Blog" (Opened at 51%).

The average user only spends about eight seconds reading an email[20]. The subject line has to achieve two things fast:

1. stand out in the inbox (e.g. I noticed it and want to open it), *and*
2. properly set up the email copy.

A misleading subject line might work once or twice, but if the subject line has no relation to the actual offer in the email, soon enough users will stop opening your emails.

Think of the open rate *holistically.* Look for ways to get more opens by:

- **Using personalization**: At the time of writing this book, only 1.4% of subject lines contained personalization.
- **Asking questions**: Questions are more engaging, and typically result in higher open rates.
- **Converting to lowercase**: Less than 1% of subject lines are entirely lowercase. Lowercase subject lines appear more natural.
- **Using emojis**: Only 2.5% of subject lines contain emojis. This will obviously change, but there are times when emojis can really help lift an open rate[21].

We'll cover more tests to run later on, but do your research first.

Come up with dozens of ideas for subject lines and run them through Send Check It[22], a free tool designed to help test subject lines. It's the best predictor for subject line success based on the data we collected[23].

If you are having difficulty coming up with good subject lines, you can download my subject line pack at saasplaybook.co/subjectlines, or use Neville Medhora's Subject Line Generator Formula[24].

The Subject Line Generator Formula gives you over 100 patterns to explore. You can even input your own topic.

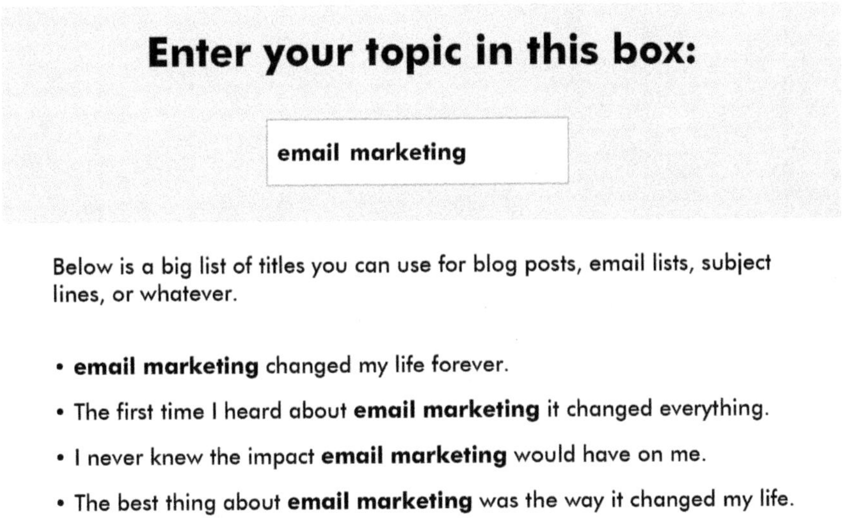

Enter your topic in this box:

> email marketing

Below is a big list of titles you can use for blog posts, email lists, subject lines, or whatever.

- **email marketing** changed my life forever.
- The first time I heard about **email marketing** it changed everything.
- I never knew the impact **email marketing** would have on me.
- The best thing about **email marketing** was the way it changed my life.

Figure 21.2 – The Subject Line Generator Formula

Through testing, you'll be able to validate if your subject lines truly perform as expected.

In the next chapter, we will look at whether or not you should be sending an email in the first place. *A bit late?* I know.

22

Does It "Really" Need to Be an Email?

By this point, you've probably figured out that I love email.

Well, in spite of my love for email marketing, not every communication needs to be an email.

In fact, there are times when emails really *aren't* the best solution. So, if not email, *what else?*

Other solutions include: In-App messages like popups, sidebars, site notifications, chat messages, browser or push notifications, desktop notifications, text messages, and even product tours and onboarding flows.

Email is great when the user *isn't* currently using your product. It's great to drive them back in, but when they are right there using your product, you can't expect them to be checking their emails at the same time.

Before setting up a new email campaign, ask yourself if email is the best way to achieve your objective and drive the user behavior you seek. Maybe a popup or site notification would be more effective.

Users can't typically unsubscribe from popups, sidebars, site notifications, chat messages, or onboarding flows. They are usually better embedded into your app and more contextual. Because of this, they tend to reach users more directly than email can. That means that they can often be more effective to influence user behaviors.

Push notifications, desktop notifications, and text messages still have some novelty to them. They can also reach users in different contexts from email.

Although sometimes it's better to use a different communication type, sometimes combining email with other options is the best way to go.

For this reason, it's important to consider the mix.

For example, an email followed on-site by an In-App message, or an onboarding flow followed by an email summing up the process may be more effective than a single email. It will allow you to follow up on user actions, and make it really clear what needs to get done.

By breaking down the steps one at a time, there's more chances for users to learn.

At LANDR, we often followed feature launch emails on-site with In-App messages. This helped to keep communications simple and goal-focused (one goal per message). The email was about getting people in the product, while the In-App message was about getting them to engage with the product.

This approach allows you to evaluate and optimize each step of the process independently.

Automation platforms like Intercom, ActiveCampaign and HubSpot generally allow you to combine messaging types.

If your platform doesn't currently have site messaging or onboarding functionalities, you may have to use multiple tools in conjunction in order to maximize results. This will make it trickier to track pacing, sequencing, and goals but it isn't impossible. You also need to consider tracking effort when adding new communication types to your mix.

As your program becomes more complex, it can be easy to lose track of the overall user experience: *Are your users getting spammed? Are you creating a disjointed customer experience?*

Test things from your users' perspective. Keep an eye out for social media messages and support requests as you do.

In the next chapter we will look at setting up automations to minimize issues and maximize outcomes.

23

Setting Up Your Automations

Once you've settled on the type of communication you would like to automate, you can get started with the setup.

Although the actual mechanics of setting up your automations will vary depending on the email marketing platform you use (MailChimp, Intercom, HubSpot, ActiveCampaign, etc), the same general principles tend to apply.

Intercom and MailChimp for example differentiate campaigns—several emails in a sequence—from one-off emails like single email *sequences*, or email blasts.

For campaigns, a trigger, or entry condition will be required. You want to understand what qualifies a user to enter this campaign.

Was it:

- *Sign up for a free trial?*
- *Trial expiration?*
- *Sign up for a paid plan?*
- *The cancellation of a subscription?*
- *A certain action that was taken for the first time (property changed from 0 to*

1, or an event happening for the first time)?
- *Did the user achieve a certain state (matched conditions or entered a segment)?*
- *Did the user do something a certain number of times (ever, or over a certain period)?* or
- *Did the user **not** do something over a certain period?*

For each automated email, you will need:

- **An audience**: *Do you send to your whole list, or to a specific segment?* There are very few situations where sending to a full list makes sense.
- **A channel**: Email, In-App, popup, push notification, etc. Depending on the platform you use, you may be limited in terms of the tools you can use.
- **A template**: *Is it mobile-friendly? Does it feel personal?* For mobile, keep both design and content concise. Screen real estate is small. You don't want people scrolling forever or waiting for heavy images to load. Have a single, very clear CTA in each email. Use simple, one-column templates.
- **Your content**: The subject line, the links, the greetings, the body copy, the UTM parameters, etc.
- **A stop date**: *Should this campaign go on forever, or do you want it to end after a month, or earlier maybe?*
- **A campaign goal**: Beyond clicks and opens, *what will tell you whether this campaign was successful? Conversions? Engagement? Other?*
- **A schedule**: *Do you want the email to trigger whenever a user qualifies for it? Day and night?* Your email will perform better if it shows up at the top of your users' inboxes after a long weekend than at the bottom with hundreds of other emails. Inboxes *do* get crowded.
- **A post-send action**: *Do users simply exit your campaign once they have received this email? Do they get tagged a certain way? Should they enter a new sequence? A new train track?*
- **An A/B test**: If you have the volume for it, it's a good idea to *always* be running some kind of test. A subject line, a send time, a CTA, or

something else.

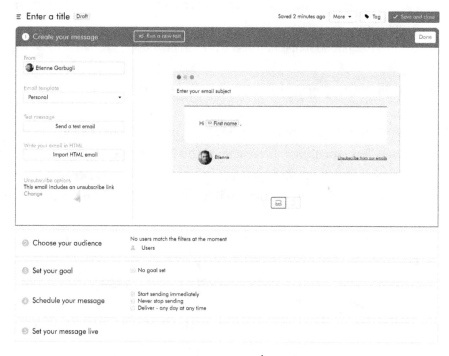

Figure 23-1 – Campaign Setup (Intercom)

Looking at implementation through these lens forces you to structure your thinking around campaign automation.

*How will this specific campaign fit within your **overall** program?*

If you just add campaigns randomly, you will wind up with email overlaps and hurt your overall engagement.

For each automation you set live, ask yourself:

Should this be the only email users receive from us on that specific day? Is it ok if the user also gets other emails (a survey email for example)?

Don't overwhelm your users. To control email volume, make sure your sequences are mutually exclusive.

For example, if users are in your onboarding sequence, make sure that they are only receiving your onboarding sequence.

For timing, use the number of days since the signup date. Segment using the time since the last email when possible. Use clear filters, for example whether the user has received such and such campaign.

Are there gaps in your automation data? Are you using first name or greeting personalization? Do all your users have those fields populated?

Plan for fallbacks. In many cases, if your segmentation relies on custom fields and the fields are not populated or have 'unknown' data, the email just won't send. You have to test your segmentation data beforehand.

Did you consider the reverse of your segments?

Segmentation recipes are either inclusive or exclusive. In either case, your automations will leave out some of your users. *Did you intend for that to happen? Do you have a fallback communication targeting the users you are leaving out?*

*Do your sequences rely on **perfect** timing?*

For example, an In-App message sequence or an email that needs to get there at a certain time, or in a certain order.

Message timing is rarely 100% accurate. Don't rely on it too much. Send emails and messages that can perform well even when one of the communi-cations is delayed.

Incorporate these rules and start setting up your automations. In the next chapter we will look at how to test emails before they send out.

24

Testing Your Emails

Early in my career, I worked for a large loyalty program in Canada. We had millions of members and were sending hundreds of thousands of emails each day. In spite of rigorous processes for testing including several in-house employees and external vendors helping implement the campaigns, we often made mistakes.

A key mistake I remember from my time in that role is when we sent hundreds of thousands of emails on behalf of a major financial institution with the wrong phone number. Worse, it turned out that the number used was the number of a local psychiatric ward.

This told me that the number was either slipped in during the review process, or that it was just terrible bad luck.

Sure, the business was able to send an apology email afterwards and change the web version of the email, but once an email is gone, *it is gone.*

No matter if you're sending a drip email, a promo, or a launch email, there's really no point in going all-in on a new and unproven email.

- If the email is meant to replace or improve an existing email, run an A/B

test, rolling it out gradually as it proves performance.
- If it's a brand-new email or a one-off campaign like a promo or a launch email, start with *pre-testing*.

This will prevent mistakes and improve the overall performance of your campaigns.

Pre-testing adds days—hours if you have enough volume—to your rollout sequences. It requires good data segmentation, but it's definitely worth it.

To do good pre-tests, you need random and mutually exclusive test groups across your entire customer journey. This will allow you to test onboarding, reactivation, or upsell emails.

The best way I found to do this is by using User IDs. User IDs are both randomly-assigned and tend to be balanced across your user base. If they are sent to your email automation platform (they should be), there will typically be 16 starting characters (0 to 9, and A to F).

3088c74f-9c3d-48c6-b6d4-5a96e14daf8e

Figure 24-1 – User ID Example

You can use those starting characters to create 16 random segments.

<u>3</u> 088c74f-9c3d-48c6-b6d4-5a96e14daf8e

Figure 24-2 – User ID Starting Character Example

Depending on the size of your audience, you can experiment with test segment sizes (1/16th, 1/8th, 1/4th, etc), or test multiple versions in parallel.

For example:

1. With a list of 10,000 users, you could start testing four offers with 625 users each;
2. Based on the response (Opens x Clicks x Goals) you could test the two best options with a fourth of your list;
3. Finally, you could send your best copy to the remaining 5,000 users.

This would allow you to build certainty and trust in your final email before send out.

It would also set appropriate expectations for performance and improve results throughout the campaign. This will help the various teams in your organization anticipate any spikes in traffic you might get.

As your audience and business grows, the expectations in terms of statistical significance—the likelihood that a relationship between two or more variables is caused by something other than chance—will increase.

Until then, being directionally accurate waiting for 100 conversions per variants tends to be good enough.

It never makes sense to send large sendouts without some level of testing beforehand.

Set yourself up for this. In the next chapter we will look at the key steps before hitting the 'Send' button.

25

Do This Before Setting an Email Live

At LANDR, the biggest mistake we ever made with email was a growth experiment gone wrong. It was a simple experiment: We were testing a one-month upgrade to a paid plan with roughly 500 users. By changing a segmentation parameter—in the segment, not even the campaign—we inadvertently sent our experiment to 85,000 users (85,000 only because we caught it on time).

The email would have easily sent to our entire user base had the engineering team not caught it early.

Because of this experiment, we had to send an apology email, do overtime support, and write custom scripts to upgrade 85,000 users at 5pm on a Friday. Needless to say, the engineering team loved us!

Mistakes happen when teams get too comfortable setting up their email campaigns. To avoid mistakes, I strongly recommend creating a pre-send routine, and reviewing it even when it feels like you know it by heart.

Before setting any campaign live, verify:

- **The segmentation**: *Who is it being sent to?* Look at random user profiles on your list—*are those the people you'd expect to reach with this campaign? Are there risks of campaign overlaps?*

- **The timing**: *When is the campaign being sent? Will it keep sending beyond the initial sendout? Will it work across time zones?*
- **The sender's name**: *Is it sent from the right person? How does the contact look in the inbox?*
- **The sender's email address**: *Does it pass spam filters? Does it look professional?*
- **The subject line**: *Does it perform well with subject line testing tools? Have any weird characters slipped in?* This is especially important for non-English communications.
- **The preview text**: *Do the expected words appear in the major inboxes?* Length varies based on email clients. 100 characters is a reasonable number of characters to put in your preview text.
- **Personalization**: *Do variables populate the right data? Do the fallback options make sense?* It's always important to have a fallback when using variable content.
- **Copy**: *Is the offer appropriate? Are there broken paragraphs? Is it error-free? Do the discount codes work?*
- **Links**: *Are the links functional? Have you added links on the images? Did you use the right tracking codes?*
- **Privacy**: *Is there an easy way to unsubscribe? Was the full required footer information included in the email?*
- **The template**: *Was the template tested across major inboxes like Gmail, Outlook, and Hotmail, and across major devices? Are there any responsive HTML issues?*
- **The goal**: *Do you have a clear way to track performance? How will you evaluate campaign performance?*

These steps may *feel* redundant, but they will save your team a lot of headaches down the road. You can use the checklist at saasplaybook.co/presend to do your own spot-checks.

You might want to add a few more subjective criteria as well. For example, I often make sure my emails are:

1. **Personal/Personalized**: I don't want to be impersonal, cold, and solely concerned with making a sale.
2. **Avoid assumptions**: I don't assume the recipient already knows the product is worth their time, or that they're immediately ready to buy.
3. **Valuable**: I focus on how the reader will benefit.
4. **Empathic/Context-aware**: I make sure each email is specific to where the user is in the user journey.
5. **Casual/Easy to respond to** (if that's the goal).

SaaS content marketer Stephanie Knapp recommends asking[25]:

- *Does it have a clear objective?*
- *Is it customer-focused?*
- *Is it attention-grabbing or memorable?*
- *Does it make sense?*
- *Is it unique?*

Come up with your own criteria.

Take note to revisit the campaign a few days after launch, checking in with support. A similar process will make sure no issues, or key feedback slips through the cracks.

Once you've gone through the list, you're ready to press send.

Let's go!!!

26

Setting Up Reporting

Surprisingly, email analytics and reporting have not evolved much in the last 10–15 years. For example, the metrics MailChimp reported on in 2006[26] are more or less the same metrics they report on today:

Figure 26.1 – MailChimp Campaign Reporting (2006)

While there have been some additions like e-commerce or goal tracking, reporting has not been the most innovative part of their business. The same applies to other email marketing platforms.

This is in part due to the limitations around email headers, the meta information included with every email you send. Email header data has stayed more or less the same the whole time through.

Businesses can get data for:

- sent;
- opens;
- clicks;
- bounces;
- unsubscribes;
- and (sometimes) deliverability.

Sadly, there are problems with the way some of these metrics are calculated.

Opens, for example, depend on a tiny pixel that gets loaded when emails are opened. If recipients don't have image-display enabled, their opens won't count.

On mobile or with Gmail, the most popular email client[27], it's often easier to open to delete an email than to just delete it. This creates a lot of false positives.

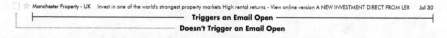

Figure 26.2 – Inbox Click Zones

Email forwards actually trigger opens, so it's completely possible for an email to have an open rate above 100%. As weird as it is, I've seen it before.

Clicks are not much better. The click rate factors in all link clicks equally. This means that clicks in the footer and clicks on your main CTA get lumped together.

Clicks are also calculated over the number of sent, not unique opens, which means that click rates can actually be quite misleading.

For example, 5% of people opening your email and clicking on your main call-to-action means completely different things if the open rate is 10% (50% of users clicked) or 90%.

On-site behaviors are rarely factored-in for clicks. Clicks with quick bounces—when the user leaves right away—also look just the same; they're not discounted or handled differently.

Unsubscribes are rarely attributed to the right emails. List disengagement is not factored in. To make a long story short, there are a lot of issues with email analytics and reporting. Keeping track of the performance of your emails can be painful.

To track email performance, you can:

- Go in your specific email marketing platform and track performance campaign by campaign.
- Export the data and create a spreadsheet for reporting (this is what we were doing at LANDR).
- Use application program interfaces (APIs) to track data and create dashboards. This will typically require some engineering time from your team.

In all cases, to get a complete picture of performance you need to combine different data sources, like on-site performance and email engagement.

You will want to move away from aggregate results (e.g. 10,000 emails sent, 30% opens, 5% clicks) towards looking at trends and performance over time. *How are your campaigns trending between dates? After the last changes you made? By segments?*

The stats you need to track for your campaigns are:

- **The send volume**: the number of people contacted;
- **The opens**: the number of people who have actually seen your email;
- **The clicks**: the number of people who took action on your offer; and
- **Goal completion**: the number of people who performed the action you were hoping they would.

On top of that, I often recommend tracking:

- **Email deliveries**: the number of emails actually delivered as a ratio of the send volume;
- **On-site bounces**: the number of people who clicked and left without even considering your offer; and
- **Replies**: If part of your goal is to get responses, or there's value in the email responses, like when asking for feedback, it can be a good idea to track those.

When you are getting started (0–20 communications or A/B tests) it will be easy to track performance directly in most email marketing platforms.

Once you get over that amount—or if you are using multiple email or notification platforms like SendGrid AND Intercom—you'll need to export the data to track specific campaigns.

As your business starts to rely on email you should use products like Highlights[28] or configure APIs for tracking.

This will allow you to get a clear picture of the full performance across certain timeframes, which will really help with optimization later on.

Unfortunately, getting a clear picture of your email program isn't easy, but with good reporting you can start getting some clarity.

Pick a timeframe (weekly, bi-weekly, monthly) based on send volume and velocity. Start measuring the relevant metrics. Track the true impact of email on your business. This will ensure that you are able to identify gaps and opportunities and to optimize the right emails.

You can use the template at saasplaybook.co/reporting to get started fast.

In the next section we will start looking at optimization specifically.

27

Tracking List Hygiene

Building your email program will cost you subscribers.

Maybe the people you'll lose didn't expect you to send them emails. Maybe they were hoping for something completely different. Or maybe they didn't appreciate one of the tests or experiments you ran. Whatever the reason, it's normal to lose subscribers when you are setting things up initially.

To avoid abuse reports and respect regulations like the EU General Data Protection Regulation (GDPR) or the CAN-SPAM act, you need to ensure that there is a one-click unsubscribe link in all your emails, transactional or not. When unsubscribe requests come through support, you should also handle them as quickly as possible.

If your emails get marked as spam too often, it will make it harder for the subscribers that *do* care about your emails to receive them. So, there is really no point in forcing people to receive your emails.

Overall, you should also monitor:

- the number of unsubscribes per list, country, and devices (web or mobile);

- your users' reasons for unsubscribing (collected by MailChimp, Active-Campaign, and many other email marketing platforms);
- the number of soft and hard bounces, which tell you whether an email address is temporarily, or permanently invalid; and
- deliverability and abuse reports.

To track deliverability and abuse reports, you can use free tools like Sender Score[29], or Litmus Spam Testing[30] and Email on Acid Spam Testing[31].

You also need to track list de-engagement (when and who becomes disengaged over time). Disengaged subscribers are like passive unsubscribers. They heavily blur your metrics.

There's an argument to be made about removing disengaged users from your email lists altogether, but I don't think it fully makes sense. It's difficult, but you can win back some of your disengaged users. We will explore a few ways to do that in the Reactivation deep dive at the end of this book.

You should track the evolution of each of these metrics over time.

You need to ensure that your unsubscribe rate remains under 0.5%[32]. If your unsubscribe rate is over that benchmark, check your users' profiles to see how many emails they receive (transactional, one-offs, and automated combined), and assess the relevance of those emails.

If email is core to your product's engagement, you could add more granular email preferences on your site (e.g. frequency, types of emails, topics, etc).

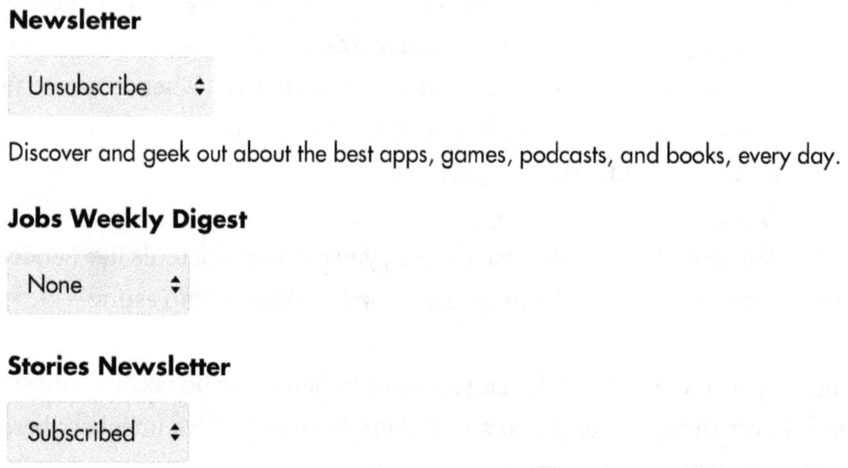

Newsletter

Unsubscribe ⇕

Discover and geek out about the best apps, games, podcasts, and books, every day.

Jobs Weekly Digest

None ⇕

Stories Newsletter

Subscribed ⇕

Figure 27.1 – Granular Email Preferences Example

Your segmentation and setup should also be trouble-checked, especially around feature releases.

It's not uncommon for product releases to break email link structures, UTM handling, or the segmentation data fed into your marketing automation platform. These issues will be hard to spot. Work with product managers and the QA team to make sure they understand your needs, and know what to look out for.

Keep an eye on these data points. If nothing else, this short list will give you areas to investigate if an issue ever arises.

28

Sourcing New Email Opportunities

As you invest more and more in your email program, you will realize that campaigns typically fall in one of four categories:

1. **Emails that perform well, or are at least "good enough"**: These emails can always be improved, but they don't need your attention at the moment.
2. **Emails that underperform**: These emails can be optimized, but if you're still in the process of building your email program, the upside of fixing them may or may not be worth your time.
3. **Emails that just don't work**: These emails don't perform for the original goal you had in mind. You either need to replace them if the email timing still makes sense, or eliminate them completely. For these emails, it's important to decide if it's kill or rework.
4. **Emails that you know you need, but didn't get a chance to add yet**: These could be new email sequences, or just additions to help correct behaviors. You can typically source these from support communications, or by looking at your analytics. We will see how in the Behavioral & Lifecycle email deep dive later on.

Categorize your existing emails in these four buckets.

Mark the emails that you'll need as *experiments*.

It will always be more costly—in terms of time and resources—to create new emails than to optimize your existing campaigns.

As you learn about your business and your email program, the gaps will become more and more obvious.

In what areas is your business struggling most:

- *Retention?*
- *Revenue?*
- *Conversions?*
- *Getting feedback?*

Can email help achieve those goals?

Would it make sense to expand your program to address those challenges with email, or through other communications?

There will always be opportunities to experiment and to grow your program if you are looking for them, but adding communications has a cost in terms of up-front effort and management.

It's best to start with the mindset: *Do we really need this?*

And question everything.

Experiment, test, and expand as you see fit.

In the next section we will look at various ways to make your emails more effective through continuous testing and optimization.

IV

Optimization

29

Why Optimization Matters

I'm a big fan of optimization.

When you optimize, a small tweak that may only take five minutes to implement can get you more money, users, or signups.

It can be one of the highest-leverage activities in a business. Not only do you get benefits short-term, those benefits can get amplified and repeated through automation.

For example, the drip sequence I put together for my book, *Lean B2B*, has been opening between 35 and 45% and clicking between 5 to 10% for three years now.

It's still not *optimal*, but it only took a few iterations to achieve those results.

In SaaS, since your users go through the same campaigns, any improvements you make at the start of the funnel improve the end of funnel as well:

- Improve your welcome email and people will want to use your product more.
- Improve your onboarding sequence and more people will experience the

value of your product and upgrade.

· Improve the quality of your upsell emails and more subscriptions will last six months or longer.
· Improve your retention sequence and maybe you can push that to two years.

At LANDR, in less than three hours per week, we were able to consistently grow results and conversions across our user base.

You can compound improvements with the right optimization process.

This is the process that I will show you in this section. The process that will help you get more with less.

Let's get this going!

30

The Problem and Limits of Benchmarks

I hate to say it, but external benchmarks for emails are useless. If you use them as guideposts for your campaigns, your emails will always underperform. Want it or not, you'll limit the potential of your own email program.

For example, MailChimp, in October 2019[33], shared that the average open rate across all industries is a little over 21%. At LANDR, only our worst campaigns opened at 21% or less. Had we based our assessments on these benchmarks, we would have never got emails that opened at two, three, or four times that rate.

The problem with these benchmarks is that they are based on the average of different types of emails, and that most businesses in your industry—or across industries really—underperform in terms of email marketing. While you can use these benchmarks as starting points, your best benchmarks will be your own performance.

This is one reason why optimization and testing are so critical.

Testing helps you uncover the *actual* limits for your business.

Maybe your welcome email opens at 21%, but it could open at 60%. This would mean three times more people in your funnel considering your product.

When we were first analyzing email data to build Highlights, we realized that comparing all emails amongst themselves gave bad results at best. For example, we had an email opening at 100% on a very low volume, a newsletter welcome email opening at 71%, and our absolute worst email opened at 18.8%.

Did it make sense to consider all of these campaigns together?

Not really.

The solution was to create groupings of similar emails.

Depending on the organization and the performance, we often saw three to four distinct groups of performance:

1. **Content upgrades and welcome emails**: The welcome email tends to be the email that gets the most opens across all businesses. Content upgrades are timely, and at the behest of prospects and users. When looking at the data, it often made sense to group these emails together.
2. **Onboarding and promo emails**: Onboarding emails follow the welcome email. As long as they remain relevant, users will want to engage. People in general tend to like sales and promos.
3. **Newsletters and regular emails**: A bit of a mixed bag. These emails tend to perform at lower rates with great variability in performance.
4. **Emails to disengaged users**: Maybe these users stopped using your product a long time ago, maybe they can't find the unsubscribe link, or maybe they no longer have access to the email address you're sending emails to. Low performance is normal for these emails.

Benchmarking against your own previous performance is the only way to get a clear picture of the potential of your email program. If one of your drip emails opens at 20%, but all of your other drip emails open at 40%, you can usually tell where the problem is.

Don't let an outside list tell you what the limits are. Go out there and find them yourself!

31

Finding (and Prioritizing) Optimization Candidates

It's not always a good idea to optimize. You have to know that an email can *reliably* allow you to reach your goals before you start thinking about optimizing it.

For example, if you're pre-product-market fit (which you shouldn't be if you are reading this book), the business drivers won't be fully clear, so you won't know what to optimize against. In that case, optimization won't be a great use of your time.

If you don't have enough volume, traffic or signups, the evaluation cycle—the time that it takes to get statistically significant test results—will be too long to get anything going. In that case, it's better to focus on traffic acquisition, first.

Optimization is useful when the business goals are clear, and you have enough traffic to iterate fairly quickly.

At this stage, do you know what to say or what to do to influence your users' behaviors to:

- *Get more conversions?*
- *Increase revenue per user?*
- *Drive more engagement?*
- *Improve retention?*
- *Get user feedback?*

Without this information, you will only be able to optimize based on basic email metrics like clicks and opens. This works, but it doesn't lead to true sustaining growth.

You can optimize an email to get amazing results, but if it's the wrong email to start with, it won't help much.

So, how do you find the right communications to optimize?

The right emails to optimize will be a mix of:

- **Volume**: If an email only sends a few times a month it's probably not worth your time.
- **Consistency**: When you introduce a new email in your program, it won't be stable. It can take time for you to find out if it works. Optimizing before knowing what you're truly dealing with is rarely a good idea.
- **Goal value**: Is the email meant to influence a key driver for your business, or is it intended to influence a secondary goal?

So, the question to ask is *which emails are most likely to influence the key business goals you're optimizing for?*:

- *Optimizing for engagement?* Focus on your welcome and onboarding sequence.
- *Optimizing for conversions?* Focus on your upgrade emails and the lead up to the email.
- *Optimizing for retention?* Focus on your upsell to yearly and your

transactional emails.

Pillar emails like these have a disproportionate impact on performance.

Slight improvements to these emails' performance will generate more results than big improvements on dozens of secondary emails.

As you get started with optimization, go through your entire program. Identify the most important emails based on your main goals.

Based on your business's benchmarks, note those with:

- worse than average deliverability (if you have the data);
- lower than average open rates;
- lower than average click rates; and
- lower than average goal rates, by tracking your entire funnel.

Emails with low open rates will be the quickest to fix. Issues with click and goal rates can take much more time to fix.

Sometimes optimization can be as simple as reordering your existing emails along the stages of the awareness spectrum (Chapter #5).

Create a list of the most important campaigns and their fixes.

We will look at what to do with each of these emails over the course of the next few chapters.

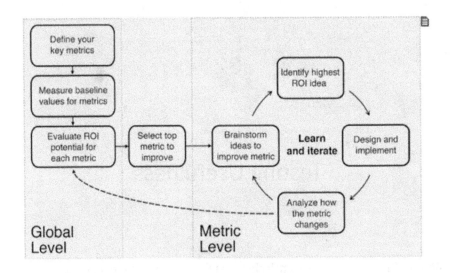

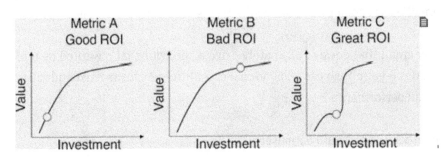

32

Testing Usefulness

With sufficient effort, it's entirely possible to get people to click the wrong email. It's probably not what you're trying to do, but it *is* possible.

Any email that doesn't ultimately drive a behavior that's wanted by both parties—your business and your users—ultimately hurts trust and future email performance.

In other words, you'll *burn* users.

You may be able to get a 50% open rate and a 15% clickthrough rate by using all the tricks and clickbaits in the book (no clickbaits in this book, sorry!). But if users land on your site and realize that they've been duped, they'll unsubscribe, they won't open your next emails, or worse, they will report your emails as spam. This then hurts future performance, game over.

The first question to ask, and you have to be honest here, is: "does this specific communication *add* to your email program?", or if you are still testing, "does it have a realistic chance of adding to the program?"

If it *doesn't*, kill it.

The best email programs have just the right number of emails driving the maximum level of engagement or return. **Sending more emails *doesn't* directly equate to getting more results from your email program.**

To understand if an email is useful, you need to look at the exact behavior driven on-site or in your app, what happens when people click a link in your email. One way to do this is via goal or micro-goal tracking, if it's an option in your email marketing platform.

Alternatively, you can use specific UTM codes for tracking. A UTM code is a string of text you can attach to a URL in order to track its traffic on-site. It looks a bit like this:

```
?utm_source=buffer&utm_medium=post-original&utm_content=-image
&utm_campaign=25-social-media-strategies
```

The key parts are:

1. **The medium**: Mediums are the Channels in Google Analytics (Referral, Organic, Social, Email, etc), or alternatively, new mediums you want to create.
2. **The source**: The Source parameter answers the question, "Where is my traffic coming from?". Google recommends using Source to describe the referrer, for example the name of a sequence like onboarding or referral.
3. **The campaign**: The Campaign parameter is the reason why the traffic is going to this page. It can be the specific goal of your email. For example, a promo name or the feature you're promoting.

You can use Google's URL builder[34] to create the UTMs you need. You should add separate UTMs to at least all the important links in your emails.

UTMs were meant to be monitored in Google Analytics[35], but nowadays, most analytics platforms (Amplitude, Mixpanel, Heap, etc) can parse UTMs as well.

To track on-site performance, you'll need Google Analytics Goals[36] or events configured.

From within Google Analytics, you can track Goals under Conversions > Goals, and Events under Behavior > Top Events.

By combining UTMs (Acquisition > Campaigns > All Campaigns) with Goals or Events as secondary dimensions you'll be able to evaluate specific results.

The question you're really trying to answer is: *Is the action being completed **as a result** of the email? Or were these people going to take this action anyway?*

If your user group truly has similar profiles—for example they're equally engaged—you can do a split test. Depending on the email volume, you can test before users receive an email against the control, when users don't receive an email. *How different is each segment's behavior?*

Looking through specific profiles and on-site actions after the email was *opened* (not just received to understand if the email content actually influenced the behavior), you'll be able to see if your communication triggers the right behavior and *adds* to your program. Even if the behavior change is very small, the email can be optimized and improved to make it more effective.

You can decide to optimize emails that have not shown the potential to perform, but usually, even a bad email will drive *some* behavior if there's volume and the content is relevant.

Don't get too attached to your emails. It's one of the main reasons why we should never *over-invest* in email design and creatives up-front.

In the next chapter we will look at optimizing for deliverability.

33

Optimizing Email Deliverability

According to ReturnPath's Email Deliverability Benchmark Report[37], 21% of opt-in emails never make it to the inbox. This means that 21% of your audience probably never hears from you. That's huge!

A lot of factors go into email deliverability (reputation, relevance, email format, send volume, spam complaints, bounce rates, blacklists, etc). Unless you are sending your emails via a transactional email platform (for example SendGrid, Postmark, or MailGun, etc), it won't be easy to benchmark yourself against that 21%. Platforms like MailChimp or Intercom will only flag major deliverability issues.

This means that you have to fully trust the platform you're using. The first important thing here is to make sure that you're using a reputable sender. There are hundreds of email platforms on the market. Unfortunately, cheaper cost often means lower standards for deliverability.

This means that your email work can be largely ineffective, but not necessarily because of the actual emails you send, or *try* to send actually.

To be proactive you can use free tools like ReturnPath's Sender Score[38] and Blocklist Lookup[39], Postmark SPAM Check[40], or Mail Tester[41] for assessment.

Litmus Spam Testing[42], Email on Acid Spam Testing[43] are also available as paid options.

I recommend doing this every month. Also think of monitoring unsubscribe abuse reports from your platform and unsubscribe rates (Chapter #27).

You can also optimize deliverability by improving the following:

1. **The double opt-in**: Double opt-in is when a user needs to confirm his or her wish to be added to your email list twice. In many parts of the world (Europe and Canada for example), double opt-in *is* the standard. Asking for a second confirmation reduces the risk of having your emails flagged as spam.

2. **The unsubscribe link**: All of your emails should have *clear* one-click unsubscribe links and often a physical mailing address in the footer. Delaying handling of unsubscribes or forcing subscribers to jump through hoops to get off your mailing list is a bad idea. It often leads in getting your emails marked as spam (the easiest way to unsubscribe).

3. **The content**: In the eyes of spam filters, words aren't created equal. To ensure delivery of your emails, avoid spammy words, ALL CAP text, and exclamation points. This is especially true for subject lines. As we mentioned earlier, there are lists[44] of spam trigger words available online.

4. **The sender's name**: A recognizable sender's name will help improve the deliverability of your emails. Again, you want to make sure that the name you use does not include spam trigger words.

5. **The sender's email address**: To help further improve deliverability, you can ask your subscribers to white-list your email address. Email whitelisting will help keep your emails out of the spam folder and improve your email's score.

6. **The email format**: Although this is certainly less true than it once was, offering both HTML and plain text versions of your emails helps improve deliverability. In fact, the lighter your emails are, the more likely they

are to be delivered.

Optimizing for deliverability is more maintenance than anything else. It makes sure that the appropriate number of people receive your emails.

In the next chapter, we will start growing our emails' performance by optimizing the open rate.

34

Optimizing Email Opens

Your email's open rate is one of the most important metrics to evaluate the performance of your email marketing campaigns. Improving your open rate is the easiest way to widen your email marketing funnel.

More people opening your emails means more prospects considering your offer. More prospects considering your offer generally means more sales and higher levels of engagement.

As mentioned before, it doesn't make sense to optimize email open rates when emails under-deliver. However, if you are ready to optimize the open rates of your emails, you'll want to aim for open rates of around 30–50%.

To do that, you'll want to focus on:

1. **The subject line**: The subject line is the element that has the most influence over an email's open rate. A great subject line can get almost any email opened. However, if the content doesn't relate to the subject line, or if the offer is irrelevant, it will damage the users' trust, and negatively impact their willingness to open future emails.
2. **The preview text**: The preview text is the first line of your email, or a hidden text element visible next to the subject line in most email clients.

It's an opportunity to create curiosity, to showcase personalization (e.g. 'Hey John'), or to highlight key email body elements.

3. **The sender's email address**: The sender's email address is the address users white-list or mark as spam. It makes sense to keep the same email address to help users white-list it. However, sometimes changing that email address can help rejuvenate under-performing campaigns.

4. **The sender's name**: A lot of experiments can be run around the sender's name: Personal vs Company, Male vs Female, Common name (e.g. Matt) vs Atypical name (e.g. Jorane), etc. Having a clear picture of your target audience can help inspire tests for different campaigns.

5. **The timing**: There are good and bad times to send email campaigns. If you think about your users' time zones and schedules (business or consumer), you can find ways to improve the timing of your email campaigns. Although platforms like MailChimp or Intercom offer automated scheduling and time zone adjustment (based on users' time zones), I've personally had more success sending emails at fixed times during the week. My go-to is 5PM EST on Mondays. Customer segmentation, and the timing within your email marketing program (e.g. send on Day 1 or on Day 10), might also impact your open rate.

To help you get started, here are ten experiments you can try:

1. Try an all-lowercase subject line (e.g. 'hello john').
2. Try scheduling your email for right before or right after your users get to work.
3. Add personalization to your email's subject line (e.g. 'John, here's an email').
4. Try sending the email *without* a subject line[45].
5. Send the email from a different email address than your usual one.
6. Try a different email preview text, making personalization visible without opening the email for example.
7. Send the email from a personal email address.
8. Use tasteful emojis in your subject line or preview text to attract the eye.

9. Add numbers, or frame your subject line as a question.

10. Re-use a tried and tested subject line, and see if it affects the open rate.

In all scenarios, you will need inspiration and a subject line tester.

Tools like Send Check It[46], SubjectLine.com[47], or Coschedule[48] are all free. They can help you create a quick feedback loop when experimenting with subject lines.

I personally use Send Check It. It's the tool that we've found to have the most accurate data[49]. It integrates with Slack and it's very easy to use. For example, if I search for 'is this thing on?', which we've used for a welcome email, I get the following:

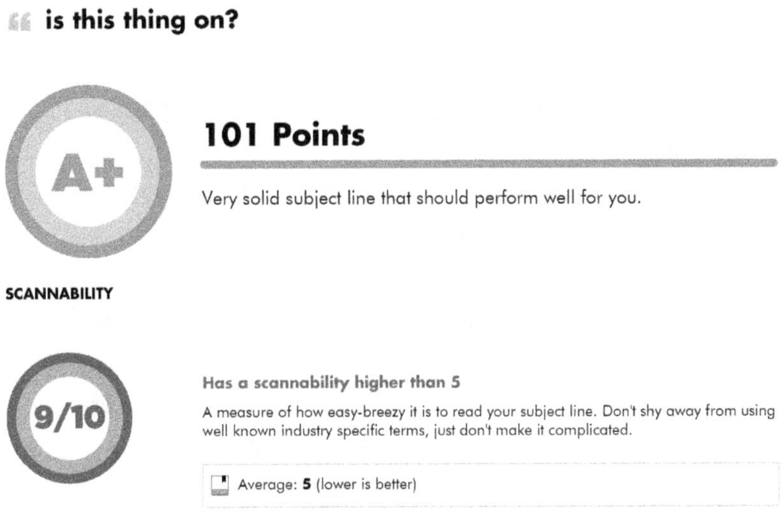

“ is this thing on?

101 Points

A+

Very solid subject line that should perform well for you.

SCANNABILITY

9/10

Has a scannability higher than 5

A measure of how easy-breezy it is to read your subject line. Don't shy away from using well known industry specific terms, just don't make it complicated.

Average: **5** (lower is better)

Figure 34.1 – Send Check It Example

Keep iterating and testing. When you are able to get good results consistently, then move on to optimizing email copy.

35

Optimizing Email Body (Offer, etc)

If your emails are getting opened and you're getting *some* users engaging with them, and you know that the content is relevant, you can improve performance by optimizing the email copy.

Depending on the call-to-action type—engagement, upgrades, etc—you can get as many as one sixth of your users clicking, responding, or engaging.

To achieve those results, you need to improve the following:

1. **The offer**: The offer is your core. Without an appropriate ask, your email will *never* work. Understand the goal of the email, and test variations. *20% off? 15% off? 10% off?* Make sure the offer is appropriate and is well-timed within your users' customer journey. You can pre-test copy with the Hemingway App[50] or Boomerang for Gmail[51].
2. **The template**: The email template helps create your user's first impression. If your template is image-heavy and under-performs, try a more personal format. Your emails are short, but don't hit the mark? Try long-form copy. If your plain text emails aren't performing, add formatting. You can pre-test your templates with HTML Email Check[52] for free, or with Litmus[53], PutsMail[54], or Email on Acid[55] if you have some budget.

3. **The greetings**: Greetings like 'Hi Sandra' are the minimum level of personalization you should be doing for your campaigns. These help to capture the reader's attention and create a base connection. You can add more personalization (city, company, use case with the product, etc), but after a certain point, personalization shows a diminishing return[56], so don't overdo it.

4. **The pull**: The pull is the first paragraph of your email. It's the introduction copy that convinces your users to read the email. If your offer, template and greetings are good, the pull is your best bet in order to increase the clickthrough rate. The pull doesn't have to be complicated. Sometimes short emails will perform really well.

5. **The CTA**: Before I started doing weekly email optimization, I thought call-to-actions had a lot of influence over clickthrough rates. It turns out that CTAs help, but they don't have a transcending impact over the performance of emails. If the offer is compelling and your users are engaged, the button label doesn't tend to matter that much. First you need to focus on driving the right behavior.

6. **The tone**: Once your email is starting to perform, you can start experimenting with the tone of the copy. Your target audience might react positively to more direct, *salesy* or casual tones. This is more of a macro-level type of optimization.

You can get started optimizing with one of the following experiments:

1. Try testing text vs button links.
2. Add a call-to-action at the top of your email.
3. Repeat the call-to-action throughout your email's copy.
4. Try adding a P.S. to your email.
5. Change the email template. Simplify. Make it feel more personal.
6. Test different versions of the first paragraph of your email to draw readers in.
7. Try a plain text email.
8. Add (or remove) visuals.

9. Use bullet points to summarize the offer, have an email summary, or use "tl;dr"[57].

10. Add personalization further down your email copy.

That's a lot to experiment with.

Email clicks often aren't enough to properly assess an email's performance. To truly understand what happens when a user engages with your emails, you have to track performance on your website or in your product afterwards.

You'll want to know if your users perform the action you want them to perform (e.g. purchase, engage, read content, etc), or if they are just leaving fast.

Optimize based on the actions taken in your product, not just clicks. Sometimes a lower clickthrough rate with more goal completions will actually be better. Optimization can get a little tricky, so look at the profiles of people converting and those that don't to find out if the behavior is what you wanted.

In the next chapter we will look at influencing the on-page behavior. Keep optimizing!

36

Optimizing Landing Pages (Page Goal, etc)

You can spend a lot of time optimizing your emails and communications, but if the supporting pages—the pages you're linking to in your product or on your site—don't perform, you will effectively be wasting time and energy.

To this end, it's often best to make sure that your supporting landing pages, conversion flows, or product UIs perform before starting to drive traffic to them with email campaigns. A rule for this is to *always* be sending users to the most efficient flow to accomplish the goal of your email.

For example, MailChimp's onboarding emails link directly to product states with pre-populated information. This helps drastically lower the friction to act for users.

At LANDR, we used to send users directly to the payment page with a pre-filled coupon code when appropriate. This performed better than sending them to the pricing page, or starting them at other points in the conversion funnel.

What you are looking for is the percentage of users that accomplish the goal when they land on this page (or state) from all channels. Then you want to compare this percentage against the percentage by channel (e.g. email vs all other channels).

If the performance via email is within your benchmark, you can direct traffic to this page with your emails.

Once you have a benchmark for your page's performance, you can start optimizing.

The first thing you need to take care of is to make sure that your page can be easily accessed; you can't get sales if your store isn't open! It's really frustrating losing sales when your site is down, or when other technical issues hold up the sales.

What you want to look at is:

1. **Page speed**: People are increasingly impatient with technology. You might lose your visitors if your app doesn't load within the first 2 to 3 seconds. You can use PageSpeed Insights[58] to benchmark your site's performance and optimize page speed. You need to look at the page size, the image sizes, the number of page requests sent, and the page elements that get stored or cached by the browser. Look at it for different segments and locations around the world.
2. **Mobile-readiness**: Since 2016 mobile browsing has exceeded desktop use[59]. Now a majority of visitors expect your pages to be optimized for mobile. Accelerated Mobile Pages (AMP) will make this even more important moving forward. Make sure your website displays well on mobile to avoid losing users and creating frustration.
3. **Trust drivers**: Your site and product need to inspire trust in order to retain users and visitors. We've all had bad surprises landing on websites with shady URLs, or sites asking to submit information or payments without proper SSL Encryption (https://... vs http://...). For $15 to 20 a year, and the price of a good .com domain name, you can avoid all of these problems completely[60].

No issues so far? Turn your attention to the core content of your pages.

I'm not going to go in details for app page flows, because these will vary depending on your app, but the following can apply to your site landing pages, pricing pages, and conversion flows:

1. **The offer**: One of the core rules of page optimization is that the page content needs to match the purpose of visit. In this case, it's clear—it's email. If the experience is inconsistent, or if the page contains multiple offers or diverging paths, the conversion rate will drop. Match the call-to-action with what *clickers* are looking for. Consider using the same words as your email copy if you know that the email performs.

2. **The main headline**: The page's main title or H1 needs to be clear and concise. Make sure it contains the appropriate keywords. You can test different keyword combinations, lengths, or stylings to attract attention. User tests, usability testing, or tools like the Five Second Test[61] can help you understand your visitors' initial reactions and understandings.

3. **The pull**: The pull is the first paragraph of your page copy. It's typically best to locate it near the headline. It should include the main benefits or clear descriptions. You can experiment by emphasizing different benefits to keep users in your app or on the page.

4. **The image/video**: Supporting images (or videos) help create an emotional response from visitors. Test different images, videos, or screenshots trying to relate with the specific segment or user demographic. Video sometimes helps improve conversion, but it's more difficult to produce. You can use heatmap tools like Hotjar[62] or Crazy Egg[63] to identify the main elements attracting your users' attention.

5. **The social proof**: Photos of customers, testimonies, logos and social media comments can all help drive conversion. Try different messages relating to your page's messaging, and try different positionings on the page.

6. **Trust drivers**: As well as a good URL and SSL encryption, trust icons (PayPal, VeriSign Trusted, etc), phone numbers, live chat, warranties,

frequently asked questions (FAQs), and clearly visible privacy policies can also help improve your conversion rate. Your users are looking for reassurance. Add trust drivers progressively and evaluate their impact on conversion.

7. **The layout**: A clean page layout, with a streamlined structure will help improve your goal rate. Eliminate unneeded page elements and experiment with the page flow (long-form vs short-form). Try to use bullet points or turn the copy into a story.

8. **The CTA button**: There's been a lot testing done around CTAs. Although buttons and links impact conversion, getting more clicks from the wrong visitors won't be very useful. If your visitors are spending time on your page and reading your content without clicking, you can experiment with larger call-to-actions, text links, different button colors (complementary or contrasting, positive or negative) or with button repetition (e.g. one button per screen or buttons following screen scroll).

9. **The supporting copy**: Different types of users will consume your page copy at different speeds. They'll also make decisions in different ways. Experiment with your sales pitch, try different proofs of benefits (case studies, quantification of benefits, etc), and lower the reading level of your copy to a grade 5 or 6. You can use the Flesch–Kincaid readability tests[64] to evaluate the effort required to read your copy.

Not all of this will be relevant. It depends on the type of page. A product page for example might have minimal copy. If it's a core landing page, it might be worth creating a page tailored to the email funnel you are creating. A general-purpose page will typically underperform when compared with a tailored landing page.

If your page has a form, consider:

1. **The form length**: Experiment with the number of form fields, or with Facebook, Twitter, LinkedIn, or Google signup to increase your

conversion rate. Don't ask for information you don't really need.

2. **The form type**: You can experiment with inline (on the page) and popup forms, and track form completion with Google Analytics. It can be effective to capture the email address upon entry to reengage visitors when they don't complete the form.

3. **The field labels**: For forms, especially lengthy forms, field label experiments can provide good results. In a long-standing research using eye-tracking devices, CX Partners demonstrated that certain form formats were more effective than others[65]. Try positioning field labels above the field, testing bold field labels, or making the labels even more scannable.

4. **The button**: The form button is usually an afterthought once the information has been entered. Again, testing different colors, shapes or labels can have an impact on conversion.

Understand the context that your email creates, and adapt communications and actions to this specific context.

Find the breakpoints, optimize by changing one thing at a time, and keep testing.

Once you are starting to get good results, it's time to move on.

37

Segmenting Successful Emails

There are two ways to improve the performance of an automated email campaign:

1. by optimizing the timing, deliverability, content, and open rate of the email, which we covered in the previous chapters; and
2. by re-segmenting it and creating targeted offers for each segment.

This is what we will cover in this chapter.

If, after all the previous optimizations, one of your key emails—welcome, upgrade, or any other—performs optimally, you can re-segment it, splitting it into different emails to further improve the results.

By sending more targeted emails:

- The benefits become clearer and more specific to each segment.
- The visuals become more effective.
- The messaging feels more personal and engaging.

Overall, this helps to create a better user experience for your subscribers and increases conversions.

So, *what segments should you use?*

As we saw in Chapter #9, there are four main ways to segment users:

- with implicit data
- with explicit data
- by user or buyer persona
- with a behavioral model

No matter which approach you choose, it's important to stick with a single segmentation model across your entire email program. This will help you avoid overlaps—sending different versions of the same email to the same people.

Although we had access to tons of explicit, implicit, and behavioral data at LANDR, we mostly relied on explicitly stated personas for targeting (i.e. vocalists, podcasters, videographers, etc). Through re-segmentation we managed to get a 78% open rate, and nearly a 25% click rate for a key reengagement email. This meant that, for a specific segment, one person out of four clicked a link in the email to access the product. This was also a 25% improvement on the open rate for the un-segmented version of the email.

If you understand the pain points, benefits and reality of the people behind your segments, you can adapt your copy to their specific needs by focusing on:

- the subject line
- the preview text
- the offer
- the specific benefits and their descriptions
- testimonies and social proof
- images or supporting visual assets

In general, you want to use the exact words that the people in your segments use to describe their pains and problems. If you don't know what those are, you can use your segments to recruit people for interviews and find out (Chapter #8).

Unless 100% of your users are covered by the segmentation, you'll need a fallback email. When a subscriber fits none of your segments, you can send them the control—the original unsegmented email.

In order to avoid a dip in performance if any of your segmented emails underperform, it's best to roll out the segmented email marketing campaigns across only a subset of your audience (20-30% at most). This will allow you to test and benchmark segmented performance against the control.

As you gain momentum and optimize the segmented emails, you can gradually increase from 30% to 50% to 80% and eventually to 100% of your subscribers.

Because re-segmentation adds overhead with multiple emails to optimize and manage, it should only be considered for key emails with steady and proven performance (think of a welcome, an upgrade, or a pivot onboarding email).

You need to factor in both the time that it takes to create the campaign and copy, and also the future cost of managing a larger email program.

At LANDR, we were sending over 300 different emails in four languages. On top of these emails, there were active discussions around adding two or three more languages. This meant that there could be as many as seven active versions of each email. Adding new emails to the core email sequences multiplied the work downstream for the team.

This is something that you should think about when optimizing through re-segmentation.

In the next chapter we will talk about the processes involved in optimization processes.

38

Recommended Processes, Team Structure, and Skillsets

Here's what happens with most email optimization processes:

- They start with great intentions.
- Resources get assigned and processes are put in place.
- Then a few weeks to a few months in, new projects derail the process.
- It becomes harder and harder to track progress and harder to get back into it.
- Eventually, they get abandoned.

To get real results with email optimization, you have to do it consistently. To make sure you can pull through, you need processes, ownership and results.

Here are a few questions to ask beforehand:

- *Who will own the process?*
- *What skills will be required?* Typically, a copywriter and an analyst will be sufficient, or maybe even just one person if the person can do both.
- *What will the evaluation cycle be? Weekly? Bi-weekly? Monthly?* It's a marathon, not a sprint. Aim for constant progress.

- *How will performance improvements be reported?* This is a ROI-generating process. This should be understood by all managers to avoid other commitments getting in the way.

There are three states for emails you'll want to keep track of:

1. **Weekly optimizations**: emails in need of improvements
2. **Currently testing**: ongoing experiments currently being evaluated
3. **Not worth testing**: communications you don't need to look at each week, but still want to keep an eye on

You should make sure you understand where every email sits within your communication program.

You also need to set up two recurring meetings:

1. A time for an analyst to assess the various tests, current performance, and prioritize optimizations by impact. This is usually best done on Mondays or Fridays.
2. A time to work on copy and improvements.

Separating these meetings gives everyone an opportunity to consider options on their own. Trying to squeeze everything in one meeting will derail your meetings, especially if it's difficult to get conclusive test results from your email marketing platform fast.

You should set your optimization meeting near peak creative productivity—in the morning for a lot of people—and out of the way of other meetings and delays.

Invite the fewest number of people possible; having more people tends to create a more distracting environment.

Stick to a plan. For example, "We optimize these ten things and then we're done."

In these meetings, you want to have the copywriter or the person writing your emails, and probably another voice maybe more in tune with the data and the software—a scrum master—to create a feedback cycle.

Make the changes during the meeting and move on.

Get wild and creative. Use sites like Really Good Emails and emails you've received for inspiration. Keep tabs for future ideas.

Since these meetings will create a lot of learnings for the organization, it's a good idea to take note of past tests (concepts, subject lines, good copy, and CTAs).

It can be useful for inspiration and sometimes to re-use subject lines that worked even though the email didn't; sometimes subject lines can be re-used in different contexts.

As you progress, communicate results and improvements to the management team. This will clarify the return on investment and make sure that resources are locked in. These meetings *should* generate a lot of ROI for your business. If they don't, get back to the drawing board and rework your process.

With the right talents, you should eventually be able to automate a lot of this process.

V

Conclusion

39

Conclusion

There's something scary about getting started with email.

Before your first campaign sends out, your email list is just that, an email list. It's pure. There are no unsubscribes. No one is responding negatively to anything you or your team wrote.

Maybe this feels good, but email addresses you don't contact don't make you money.

Here's how to get over the hump:

Afraid to say the wrong thing?

Start small. Test your messaging on a small segment. Get a feel for the tone and voice before expanding.

Afraid of 'burning' through your list?

How many bad emails do you actually remember? Maybe you'll receive *some* negative feedback, but you'll never burn through your entire list. Don't believe it!

Not sure?

Start safe and don't be too pushy until you feel comfortable being a bit more pushy.

Afraid of spamming your users?

There is no clear relationship between the number of emails a brand sends and the number of unsubscribes it gets.

Both Pinterest and Product Hunt send emails daily. But they are still two brands that people love.

People don't unsubscribe because they receive too many emails. They unsubscribe when there are too many *unwanted* messages. As long as your emails are relevant, you can send more emails than you feel comfortable about sending.

Afraid your emails won't perform?

Ship faster. Testing is the best way to find out if your copy or concepts will fly. The reality is, if you're not contacting your users, then you are *already* burning through your list.

We've all received emails from sites and services that we signed up for ages ago but that only just got started with email. What's our reaction in those cases?

Confusion? Unsubscribes? Worse? Don't be those brands.

With email, *done is better than perfect.*

You'll only be successful if you can live with temporarily imperfect emails.

The best time to start with email would have been yesterday, but if you start today you will be able to get predictable results from email in the near future.

Let's get to it!

VI

Deep Dives

40

Cold Email Sequences

Cold emails get a bad reputation, and it's easy to see why.

We've all received generic emails with little to no personalization, with too many links, asking us to take irrelevant actions.

But the truth is that, done well, cold emails can be a great way to acquire new customers in SaaS.

The problem is that many businesses think cold emails are about sending emails (a lot of them), when cold emails are really more about research: precisely understanding and finding the right prospects, and then introducing them to your product.

Ever since companies like Salesforce[66], Zenefits[67], and Birchbox[68] demonstrated that cold emails can help build billion-dollar companies, brands of all kinds have turned to cold emails to acquire customers.

This makes sense. After all, everyone spends 1–10 hours a day in their inbox. Thanks to mobile phones, emails can be retrieved anywhere, on the go. And everyone needs solutions to their top one or two biggest problems. Done well, cold emails can help reach the right people at the right time with the right offer.

The key words there are *done well*. With thousands of SaaS vendors globally relying on cold emails for growth, your emails have to cut through the noise if they are going to capture the attention of your prospects.

So, when should you use cold emails?

I've used cold emails to get customer interviews, recruit employees, land guests for podcasts, and drive sales. Cold emails can be instrumental in helping achieve many business goals.

In SaaS, the goal of cold emails is to start conversations, or get meeting with prospects. They are much better for opening discussions than for closing sales.

Because of the costs involved in doing research, creating email scripts, and following up with prospects, it is easier to make cold emailing work in B2B, or for the promotion of high-ticket B2C items like insurance or financial services.

1. Setting Up Your Inbox

The first rule of cold emails is to never send emails from your work inbox.

Gmail, for one, has been improving its algorithms trying to reduce the number of unwanted cold emails. If your account is reported too often, your email address, or worse, your domain could get flagged. If that happens, it's game over. Trust me, recovering from a flagged email account is quite painful!

To get started, buy a new domain. Consider acquiring a domain that is very similar to your company URL, perhaps simply with a different domain extension.

To set up your inbox afterwards:

1. Fill out your profile, and complete it with your mailing address.
2. Add a profile picture.
3. Create an email signature that includes the full address.
4. Sign up to 20+ newsletters to start emails flowing through your inbox.
5. Email 10+ friends (not colleagues), having them reply to your emails.

Your inbox needs to look and feel as real as possible in the eyes of Google and other email providers. You need to start slow, sending, at most, 50 emails per day.

2. Finding Email Addresses

To be effective, your cold emails must be relevant, and relevance is a *who-what* pair.

At this stage, you should know who typically purchases your product within organizations: *Is it product managers? engineers? Chief Financial Officers? another role maybe?*

Unless you have learned differently, it's usually best to target the people who buy your product. They're the ones who will be most likely to see the value of your offering.

If you aren't sure who that is, it's useful to know that founders are typically the best point people for companies under 100 employees, while relevant director-level executives make the best entry points for organizations between 100 to 250 people[69].

There are lots of ways to find prospects online. You can use LinkedIn,

LinkedIn Sales Navigator, professional association directories, or any other watering holes to build your prospect lists. Once you have a list of 50+ names, companies, and other relevant information, you can use tools like Hunter[70], ZoomInfo[71], Voila Norbert[72], or Clearbit Connect[73] to quickly find your prospects' email addresses.

I personally use Clearbit Connect. It's a browser extension that sits inside Gmail. It gives you 100 free credits per month, and is 97% accurate according to research by YesWare[74]. Using it is as simple to use as typing an organization's domain name, searching for the name of your prospect, and copying their email address.

3. Researching Prospects

A major difference between cold emails and the emails you send to your subscribers is the fact that cold email recipients have little to no context on your company. They didn't sign up to your list, they don't know you, and they may have never heard of your company.

It's important to establish rapport to get them to, at least, consider your email.

One way to do this is through personalization.

To make your campaigns successful, you have to spend time researching your prospects one by one. You can't skip this step; it's what ultimately separates your emails from the spammers'.

At the very least, you should include:

- the recipient's first name; and
- a custom lead-in.

Making your personalization visible from the ledger in the inbox will help increase the open rate for your emails.

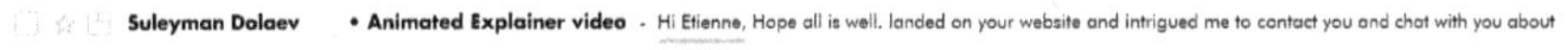

Figure 40.1 – Visible Personalization in the Inbox

The lead-in can be anything that helps establish rapport with the prospect. It's a way to show that you have done your research and to start a conversation.

Here are a few things you can comment on, ranked from most to least effective:

1. **Personal success**: a job promotion, an award, an achievement
2. **Company news**: related to them, their department, or a significant company achievement like a fundraising event
3. **A shared experience, acquaintance, hobby, or interest**: ideally something beyond work
4. **Recent posts**: on LinkedIn, Medium, or on their own blog
5. **Company accomplishments**: 5-star ratings, reviews, releases, etc
6. **Recent LinkedIn or Twitter updates**

It's recommended that you change at least 20% of the email content from one prospect to the next.

You can add more personalization, but don't overdo it. After a certain point, adding more personalization no longer increases the response rate[75]. Even worse, it can actually make your emails feel creepy.

4. Writing the Cold Email

Nailing the cold email script will make a huge difference in your response rate.

As already mentioned, prospects have none of your company context at this stage. You can't assume that they care about you, or your business.

Your email has to be short—ideally less than five sentences. The tone should be casual. You are simply a normal person trying to help another person by showing them a great software solution.

Make it about them. Avoid "I" and "we". Use more "you".

Don't use acronyms, bullet points, or full company names (e.g. Stripe Ltd.).

The cold emails that get responses are ones that feel natural and personal. They are short and to the point.

Make your emails easy to respond to.

Instead of asking for meetings right away, try direct calls-to-actions like:

- "Is this a priority for you this quarter?
- "Are you the best person to speak to about this?"
- "Is this worth looking into?"

A few subject lines you can try include:

- [General Topic]
- [Company Name] and [Company Name]
- Quick question
- Hi from [First Name]

- [Compliment]

Here's a sample script you can use:

International Growth

Hey [First Name],

[I enjoyed your 2-part series on employee retention. I had tried to find a job with startups in Hong Kong when I was living there and I know it's not easy.]

I'm head of growth for [Your Company] - our product helps businesses find leads internationally. With our product, you could find highly targeted contacts at companies that would find value in [Company].

[Your Company] helps with outreach, call scheduling, and closing.

Is this worth looking into?

Let me know, thank you.

[Your First Name]

Figure 40.2 – Cold Email Example

Feel free to adapt the email script, or use it as inspiration.

Note that if you're targeting European businesses, you must include unsubscribe links in your emails.

5. Sending/Testing Your Cold Emails

Once your prospect list and your cold email script are ready, you can start sending cold emails.

You could decide to send all emails manually (a lot of low-value work), but you'll be better off using cold email software like Mailshake[76], YesWare[77], or Streak[78]. These tools will allow you to send true plain-text emails, manage contacts and campaigns, and track email and A/B test performance.

I personally use Streak[79]. It's a CRM that sits inside Gmail. It allows you to send mass personalized emails, manage pipelines, track replies, send follow-ups, and schedule email delivery right from your inbox. And it works well in conjunction with Google Sheets.

As with any other email campaign, you should do tests before sendout. You can refer back to Chapter #25 for the email pre-send testing process.

Schedule your emails carefully. Ask yourself: *Where are my prospects located? At what time do they get up? Go to work? When are they likely to have time to look at our emails?*

Start slow. Don't send too many emails (you need time to reply). Send batches of ten emails to test different subject lines before speeding it up.

CEOs and many business executives live in their inboxes. If that's who you're targeting, you will most likely be able to get most of your campaign's results in a day or two.

For the first email of your sequence, you're looking for open rates of 60–85%, with bounce rates under 10%, and a response rate of 20% or more.

Cold email open rates often have more to do with deliverability than the subject lines you are using. Start there if your open rate is well under 50%.

6. Following Up

According to Reply.io, 66% of replies happen after the first email, and roughly 20% of all replies happen after the third email[80]. In short, if you're not sending follow up emails, you're missing most of the action.

Keep your emails casual. Don't sound annoyed by the lack of response. People are genuinely busy, and most people do take vacations.

It's a good idea to follow up at least seven times.

Your goal is to get to a clear "Yes" or "No". As Close.io CEO Steli Efti says: "*Maybes* kill startups."

You can set a simple follow-up schedule like this one:

- Day 1: First follow up (+2);
- Day 3: Follow up (+4);
- Day 7: Follow up (+7);
- Day 14: Follow up (+14);
- Day 28: Follow up (+30);
- Day 58: Follow up (+30);
- Day 88: Follow up (+30).

Here are a few examples of follow-up emails I often use:

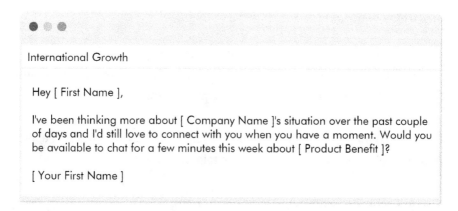

Figure 40.3 – Cold Email Followup Example

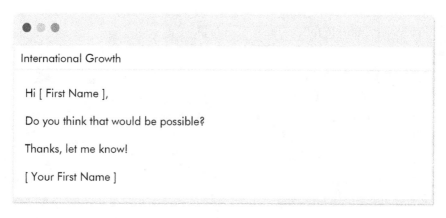

Figure 40.4 – Cold Email Followup Example

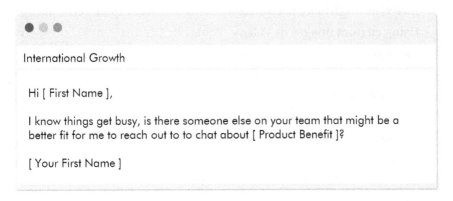

● ● ●

International Growth

Hi [First Name],

I know things get busy, is there someone else on your team that might be a better fit for me to reach out to to chat about [Product Benefit]?

[Your First Name]

Figure 40.5 – Cold Email Followup Example

Optimize your cold email sequences using the processes discussed in the fourth section of this book.

Test your deliverability weekly. If you realize that your open rates are dropping, it's possible that your account got flagged.

If that's the case, unfortunately you'll have to re-start from the top.

Once you have found your style and a level of success, consider:

- **Warming up prospects before sendout**: Often times, interacting with prospects before first contact can help warm up the lead. This can be done on social media by liking, commenting, or sharing posts on Twitter, LinkedIn, or Facebook, commenting on or sharing blog posts, or displaying targeted ads based on your prospect lists[81].
- **Targeting site visitors**: Growth advisor Guillaume Cabane helped define the *Reveal Loop*[82]. The general idea is to use tools like Clearbit Reveal[83] or Leadfeeder[84] to identify the companies visiting a website based on their IP addresses. Based on the behavior on-site and interests, a business can

then send much more relevant cold emails and warm up the relationships.

· **Using custom images or videos**: Tools like Lemlist[85] and Loom[86] can allow you to include custom emails and videos in your cold emails. Although the novelty of custom images or videos will certainly fade, done tastefully custom assets can help capture the attention of prospects, and get your cold emails answered.

· **Scaling through on-demand workers**: Once your cold emails are starting to perform and your team is starting to hone its processes, it can be a good idea to start delegating some of the research work to interns or on-demand workers on Upwork[87] or Fiverr[88]. Although you probably want to keep writing the lead-ins and sending the campaigns yourself, those workers can help you find emails and build prospect lists fast.

● ● ●

[First Name], watch this video of how Intercom's Product Tours could work for you

Hi [First Name],

Chantal from Intercom here. I want to show you how you can use Intercom's Product Tours for highlights to turn new sign-ups into successful customers.

With Product Tours, you'll be able to:

- **Create interactive tours** that onboard new customers, spotlight new features, or give customers proactive guidance.
- **Build tours code-free** with our easy-to-use visual interface that includes quick-start templates.
- **Access powerful and purposeful features** like click-to-advance progression, multipage tours, and embeddable links to share tours anywhere.

Click here to watch the video and let me know if you'd like to learn more.

Cheers,
Chantal

Figure 40.6 – Intercom's Feature Launch Email

Cold emails can be a great way to acquire new SaaS customers.

As you grow, scale your research before attempting to scale your send volume.

There will always be the temptation to send emails without doing proper research. Resist the temptation. Your campaigns will be a lot more effective for it.

41

Welcome & Onboarding Sequences

The goal early on is to quickly establish your product's value by getting users to their desired outcomes.

The people signing up to use your product already have a certain idea of what your product does—or at least what it *should* do for them—when they sign up. This idea is what customer success expert Lincoln Murphy calls the desired outcome[89]; what users *hope* your product does for them.

Your goal is to help new signups discover the product value and experience their Aha moment: the moment of realization of value, when they figure out that your product addresses their needs. The faster you can convince them that your product is valuable, the faster you will create engaged and happy subscribers.

To do that, you need to: 1) identify the *must-have* experience in your product; and 2) look for ways to front-load that experience[90].

So, *what drives the Aha moment?*

Activation, or the activation rate, is the metric that is most often associated with a user's Aha moment. It's also the metric which ultimately has the most influence over conversion and long-term retention in SaaS[91].

The better users understand the value of your product, the more likely they are to use it, to come to depend on it, and to be happy to pay for it—and to keep paying for it.

The problem with activation and activation metrics is that, unlike most of the other pirate metrics like acquisition, revenue, or referral, your activation metric will be unique to your product and your business. In other words, you need to find what drives the Aha moment for your product.

I originally found LANDR's activation metric by spending days comparing retention cohorts looking at different actions that users took in the product: people who do *this* action have *this* level of retention; while people who do *that* action have *that* level of retention, etc.

Thankfully, analytics tools like Amplitude now have built-in functionalities to help get such data quickly. They do this by calculating correlation coefficients—the strength of the relationship between two variables—across all user actions and behaviors.

For example:

- users who purchased a subscription AND connected their account to Facebook; or
- users who purchased a subscription AND used the product daily.

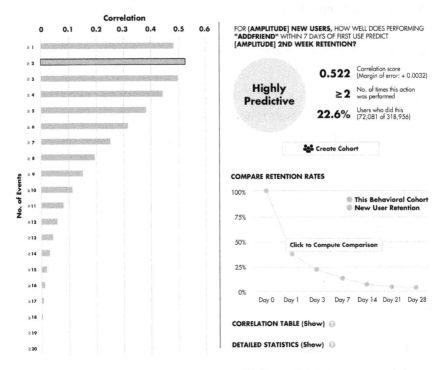

Figure 41.1 – Compass by Amplitude

For LANDR, we eventually found that a certain number of song masterings had the highest correlation with long-term product use and retention. A year later, we ran the analysis again and came to the same conclusions.

The same analysis can allow you to uncover which of your product's features are most correlated with conversion, retention, or any other goal. It can help you map and sequence your Aha moments, which is what you want to do for onboarding.

For example, if your product was a smartphone, your Aha moments might be:

1. quick setup

2. calendar and email sync
3. camera quality
4. video content suggestions

Helping new users discover these features would help them realize just how valuable and essential a smartphone can be to their work, or personal life. This concept is sometimes called the Minimum Path to Awesome (MPA)—the optimal path to value discovery in your product.

Ideally, if your acquisition flows—your ads, landing pages, and CTAs—set the right expectations, the transition to onboarding and product usage will be seamless.

Wes Bush recommends differentiating between two types of communications at this stage:

1. **Product bumpers**: tours, checklists, tooltips, In-App messages, or progress bars—which help users in the application itself; and
2. **Conversational bumpers**: emails and sales outreaches—which prompt users to come back to the product.

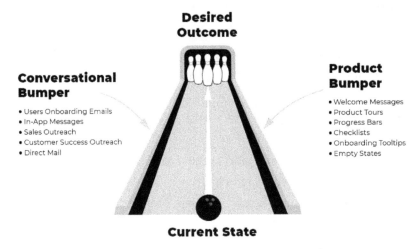

Figure 41.2 – Product Bumpers vs Conversational Bumpers

Both types of communications have to work hand-in-hand.

If you have on-site onboarding—welcome messages, coachmarks, or a product tour—you need to ensure that it tells a single, coherent story.

1. The Confirmation Email

Many businesses will start their email program with an email address confirmation email. Although those emails can be useful when a lot of new users have invalid email addresses, they're rarely worth the friction they introduce. Users are signing up to use your product. They are starting to discover your product's functionalities. Asking them to leave your product, open their inbox, and click a link to come back to your product adds little value for them. It's also a major lost opportunity.

At LANDR, we didn't actually need a confirmation email, but we kept sending one because, more than the other *more sophisticated* emails we tried, the reminder (the big green button at the center of it, really) drove people back into the product. And when they came back, they performed the actions we wanted.

Confirmation email or not, it's important to test and weigh the alternatives to figure out the best strategy for your business.

2. The Welcome Email

Now, whether the experience starts with a confirmation email or not, you should have a welcome email to help drive momentum and reinforce your users' decision to try your product. You want users to know that they made a great decision!

There are different approaches to welcome emails. But the general idea is to reinforce the signup decision and build forward momentum by setting the expectations for what's coming next.

This can be done through:

- a personal reachout opening the door for support, "Hey I'm Etienne, thanks for signing up, don't hesitate if you have any questions";
- driving the user to try the single most important functionality (which should lead to the main Aha moment);
- providing an overview of the product's benefits; or
- showcasing a certain product use case.

Since welcome emails get more opens than almost any other emails—four times the total open rates according to Experian[92]—you want to be sure that they set the right tone and drive the right behavior, sending users on their way to activation.

Every welcome email should have a specific goal, for example:

- "Download the app ... ";

- "Connect your account ... "; or
- "Import your data ... ".

Don't waste this important opportunity!

Research by SeeWhy[93] suggests that businesses have a window of 90 minutes before leads go cold. So send your welcome email as soon as users sign up. Use the momentum to get users to further their engagement with your product.

3. The Onboarding Emails

Depending on your product's natural usage cycle *without* email you can follow the welcome email with a series of onboarding emails sent on the days when product usage tends to dip.

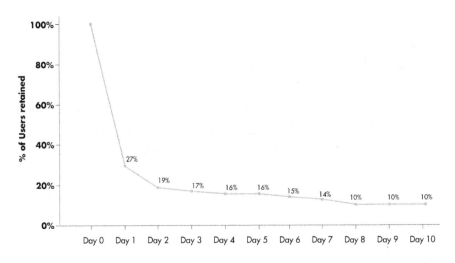

Figure 41.3 – Retention Curve Timing

For example, looking at the above retention cohort, you could decide to send your onboarding emails on days 2, 4, 8, and 12 leading up to an upgrade email, trial or not.

Onboarding emails are about:

- moving users closer to their desired outcomes;
- creating the habit of using your product;
- helping users experience product value so that they, eventually, become paid subscribers; and
- reducing the friction of using your product.

Onboarding emails are an extension of your product. They have to bridge the gap between your users' desired outcomes and the value they will get from using your product.

This is often done by demonstrating the product value through:

- use cases;
- benefits; and
- case studies or customer stories.

Since the first few emails will get the most opens, and users typically won't open all of your emails, it's a good idea to front-load your series with your best arguments—the value drivers with the most potential to get your product used (and your emails opened). To accelerate sales and increase conversions, you have to be aggressive with your emails in the first days of the user lifecycle.

Highlights actually has two similar but distinct sequences: one for agencies, and one for bloggers, solopreneurs, and in-house marketing teams (but I really wouldn't recommend splitting up your efforts this way until a single sequence shows great returns).

The welcome email, onboarding sequence, and upgrade emails were set up before launch. These were based more on assumptions than hard data, which led to a lot of re-sequencing, changes, and the need for optimizations. This will most likely be the case for your sequence as well.

For Highlights, the welcome email is followed by four onboarding emails leading up to an upgrade email sent on day 13, one day before the 14-day trial ends.

The Aha moments are:

1. simple interpretation of analytics;
2. custom prioritization;
3. automatic prioritization; and
4. global overview.

As users experience specific Aha moments, it's a good idea to change the emails you send, so that they get to experience the next most important benefits.

Different users will learn and get started at their own pace. Using action-based or behavior-based emails, tied to what users are doing in your product, can be very effective at driving users to the next most valuable elements in your product.

Let's take a deeper look at Highlights' Welcome & Onboarding sequence.

Welcome Email (67% Opens, 10% Clicks)

The welcome email reinforces the product's key benefit. It uses personalization, and has a clear CTA. This email asks users to perform a small, but essential task that is necessary to allow them to experience the product value.

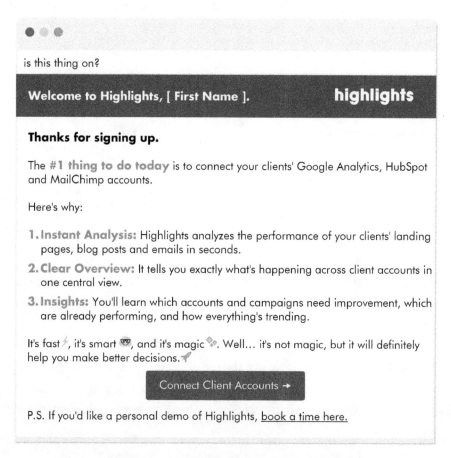

Figure 41.4 – Highlights' Welcome Email

Onboarding Email 1 (46% Opens)

The goal of the first onboarding email is to open the door to support. The general idea is to humanize a fully automated service.

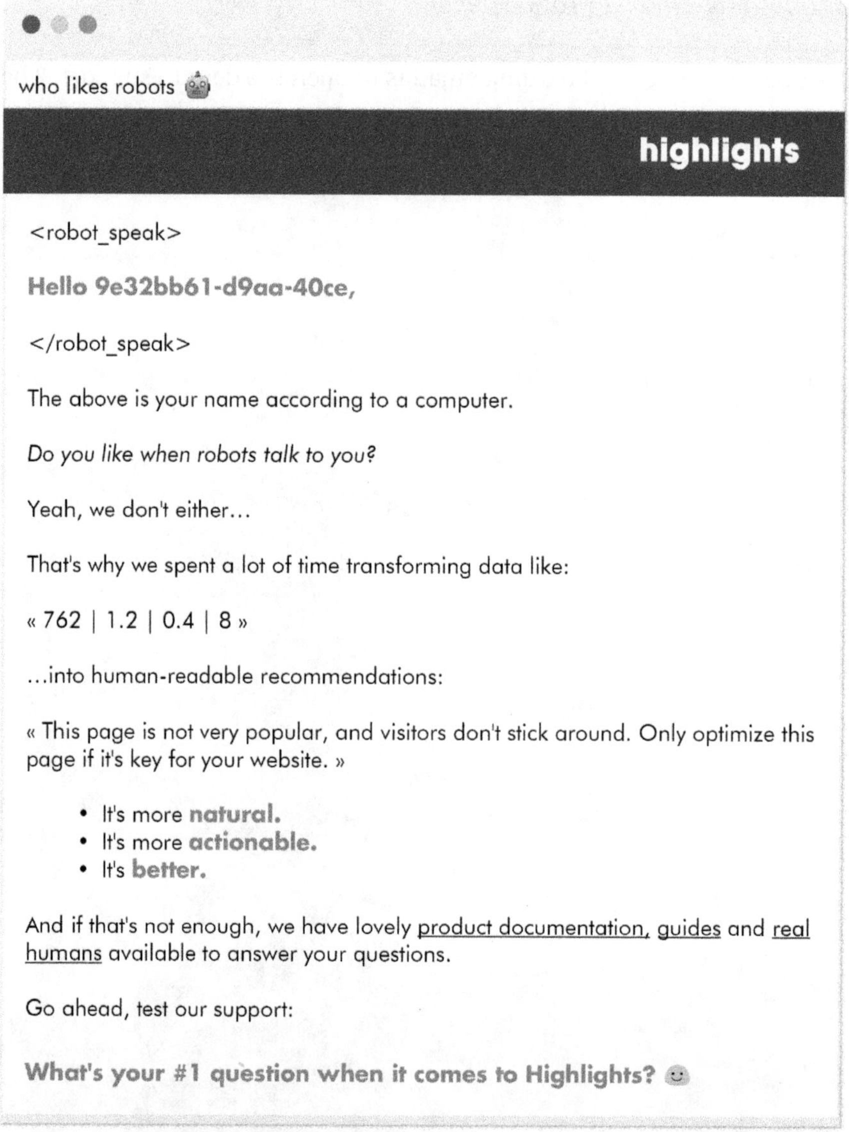

who likes robots 🤖

highlights

<robot_speak>

Hello 9e32bb61-d9aa-40ce,

</robot_speak>

The above is your name according to a computer.

Do you like when robots talk to you?

Yeah, we don't either...

That's why we spent a lot of time transforming data like:

« 762 | 1.2 | 0.4 | 8 »

...into human-readable recommendations:

« This page is not very popular, and visitors don't stick around. Only optimize this page if it's key for your website. »

- It's more **natural.**
- It's more **actionable.**
- It's **better.**

And if that's not enough, we have lovely product documentation, guides and real humans available to answer your questions.

Go ahead, test our support:

What's your #1 question when it comes to Highlights? 😊

Figure 41.5 – Highlights' Onboarding Email 1

Onboarding Email 2 (38% Opens, 5% Clicks)

The second onboarding email showcases custom prioritization by asking the user to perform a quick task. It both creates and leverages a knowledge gap. The P.S. helps reinforce the main CTA.

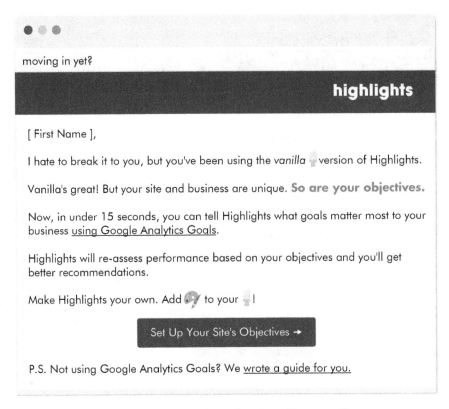

Figure 41.6 – Highlights' Onboarding Email 2

Onboarding Email 3 (36% Opens, 10% Clicks)

The third onboarding email leverages curiosity to get users back in the product. The open rate needs a bit of work on this one.

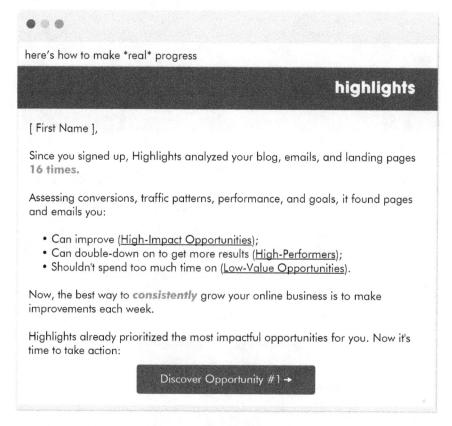

here's how to make *real* progress

highlights

[First Name],

Since you signed up, Highlights analyzed your blog, emails, and landing pages **16 times.**

Assessing conversions, traffic patterns, performance, and goals, it found pages and emails you:

- Can improve (<u>High-Impact Opportunities</u>);
- Can double-down on to get more results (<u>High-Performers</u>);
- Shouldn't spend too much time on (<u>Low-Value Opportunities</u>).

Now, the best way to *consistently* grow your online business is to make improvements each week.

Highlights already prioritized the most impactful opportunities for you. Now it's time to take action:

Discover Opportunity #1 →

Figure 41.7 – Highlights' Onboarding Email 3

Onboarding Email 4 (52% Opens, 10% Clicks)

The final onboarding email is short and to the point. It uses personalization mid-copy and repeats the CTA. Performance went back up for this last email.

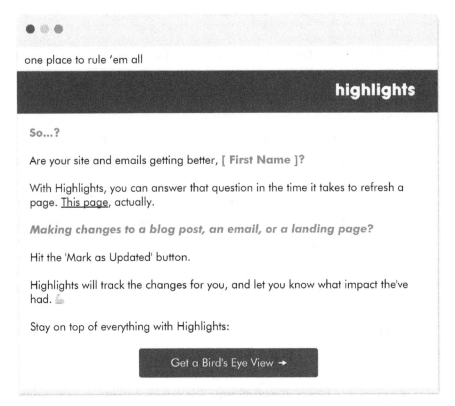

Figure 41.8 – Highlights' Onboarding Email 4

Is this sequence perfect? No.

There is still a lot of room for growth and optimization, but it's *good enough* for now.

A few things to consider as you set up your Welcome & Onboarding sequence:

- **One email, one CTA**: Focus each email on a single ask. Use your call-to-actions to re-enforce product value.
- **Deep links as much as possible**: Try to link as far as possible inside your product. Use direct links. Keep in mind that some of your users will need to log in.
- **A matter-of-fact tone helps build trust**: Get to know your users before starting to get too funny with your brand or messaging.
- **Don't be too pushy:** Everything's going well at this point. Don't be too pushy early on.
- **Open rates will decrease**: It's normal for open rates to decay after your welcome email. The important thing is that your sequence sustains a base level of performance.
- **Email pacing is more art than science**: Until you start testing, you won't be able to get conclusive evidence as to how fast (or how slow) your sequence should be.

Consider under-scaling your onboarding, and starting with a manual process to learn from your user base. As Andrus Purde, founder of Outfunnel says[94]: "It's a good idea to do something manually for long enough before you start automating".

Users, especially in B2B, value proximity. It's one of the reasons why sales-assisted onboarding—when salespeople contact freemium leads—converts almost 3.5 times more than self-served onboarding[95].

A typical pattern for email onboarding is to send a welcome email at the time of signup, following it up the next day with an onboarding email, then sending emails every other day.

The important thing is to start from the top and start testing. Once your welcome email starts driving product engagement, then add your first onboarding email. Once that first onboarding email also increases engagement, add the next email, and keep going.

At LANDR, we found that if users didn't become active within the first 90 days, less than 2-3% ever really became engaged with the product. Because of this, it made sense to keep expanding the product value well beyond the upgrade email.

Research by MadKudu[96] has shown that it takes about 40 days to get 80% of SaaS conversions. For most businesses, half of conversions will happen after the trial ends. And as Tomasz Tunguz, managing partner at Redpoint Ventures, demonstrated in a report based on 600 SaaS businesses, the conversion rate is the same across trial lengths[97].

This makes sense. Sam Levan, Co-Founder & CEO of MadKudu, explains[98]: "A free trial creates artificial purchasing urgency. But there isn't anything magical about the last day of a trial—some customers continue to convert at their own rate based on incentives or their perceptions of value."

The first 30-40 days of your user cycle are crucial[99]. But you definitely want to follow up for the first 90 days after signup, well after the trial ends. As long as your onboarding emails add to the overall performance and usefulness of your series, you can keep adding and pushing for activations.

As already mentioned, MailChimp sends 11 onboarding emails. You may want to change the tone once the trial is over, but it's well worth continuing to push for engagement.

Let's get your users onboard!

42

Behavioral & Lifecycle Emails

A lot of things go into a conversion rate, an activation rate, or a churn rate. Some users will reach a milestone without any issues, while some will get stuck at critical stages.

This is the great power of lifecycle and behavioral emails: they can help support or influence users at key stages to improve overall usage and performance.

Sometimes behaviors or issues will be too specific to change the product interfaces, or sometimes it won't be easy to get engineering time to fix certain issues. In those situations, behavioral emails and In-App messages can make a big difference in helping improve usage and conversions.

Let's look at it from Highlights' perspective. At a high level, the funnel[100] looks like this:

Figure 42.1 – Highlights' Funnel

The overall goal is to get users to activate—that is several clients, and several weekly uses—in under a week.

Although this high-level funnel gives you a good overview, it can be highly misleading. There are actually many sub-steps a level below where usage breaks down.

If we take a closer look at the flow:

1. Users either get acquired through search, content marketing, or via cold emails.
2. They sign up from the blog, the home page, the pricing page, or sometimes random pages like the Terms & Conditions.
3. They can drop off at any one of the three steps of the setup process.
4. When they do reach the home screen after those three steps, the results sometimes vary.

Already, that's dozens of different contexts and experiences.

More decisions mean more breakpoints. That's not necessarily bad, but it makes for more complex customer experiences.

Based on the data, you can identify the drop offs:

	Week 1	Week 2
Users in Cohort	1000	1300
Acquisition		
Visits the blog	100.0%	100.0%
Clicks a link to the homepage	15.0%	13.8%
Clicks the signup button	2.5%	2.5%
Begins signup process	2.0%	1.8%
Completes signup	1.7%	1.8%
Visitor is considered Signed Up	17	23
Activation		
Views 1st step of onboarding process	1.7%	1.8%
Completes 1st step	1.6%	1.6%
Completes 2nd step	1.3%	1.4%
Completes 3rd step (optional)	1.2%	1.2%
Accesses the main interface	1.2%	1.2%
User is considered Activated	12	15
Retention		
User comes back to the product	0.6%	0.7%
User uses the product 3 times	0.3%	0.5%
User is considered Retained	3	6

Figure 42.2 – Highlights' Funnel Drop Offs

Once you have identified a breakpoint in your conversion funnel performance, you should analyze it from all angles:

- *Do users from different traffic sources behave differently?*
- *Are there countries, regions, or cities that perform better than others?*
- *Can users on mobile, tablet, or desktop complete the same tasks?*
- *Were there considerations in terms of site performance?*
- *Were there issues with payment, or anything else you haven't foreseen?*

Similar analyses can tell you about the context and the scope of considerations.

Is it more about the user, the context, or is something broken? If it's the user, then you can communicate with different segments differently. If it's the context, you can give pointers, or open the door for support. If something is broken, you can find an alternate path to get users over the hump.

From there, consider the best path to influence behaviors: *Are they in the app when the issue is happening?* Then consider In-App messages. *Are they off-site after the issue happened? Can you anticipate the issue?* Then consider email.

Don't expect perfect timing. Chances are that the behavioral messages you put in place will reach the user *after* the issue occurs.

Get creative with your targeting and segmentation.

Run tests. It will sometimes be difficult to reproduce certain issues, but you can test to figure it out.

Pick the right tone. Helpful usually works best when dealing with issues. Slightly more pushy works best for behavior bumps.

Make sure the communications you set up work well with the other sequences in place. A single email can usually be squeezed in within a sequence, but if multiple messages are required, you might need to divert to a new train track.

Focus on the issue, and make sure you don't overwhelm the users.

At Highlights, we ended up setting up three behavioral campaigns:

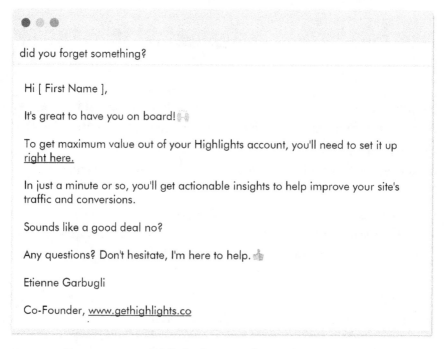

did you forget something?

Hi [First Name],

It's great to have you on board!

To get maximum value out of your Highlights account, you'll need to set it up right here.

In just a minute or so, you'll get actionable insights to help improve your site's traffic and conversions.

Sounds like a good deal no?

Any questions? Don't hesitate, I'm here to help.

Etienne Garbugli

Co-Founder, www.gethighlights.co

Figure 42.3 – Highlights' Incomplete Onboarding Email

1. **Incomplete onboarding on Day 1**: If a user has signed up, but hasn't completed their onboarding, they get an email (usually they're no longer in the app). Instead of overwhelming them with a series of tasks to perform, call-to-actions cascade from most to least urgent based on which actions the users has taken in the product. *No user type selected? Email sent. User type selected, but Google Analytics not set up?* The above email gets sent. *Incomplete Google Analytics setup?* Different email—and so on.

2. **Completed onboarding on Day 1**: If a user has completed the onboarding process, a personal follow-up email gets sent from me, the original founder. The email welcomes the user, opens the door for questions, and uses the P.S. to make a targeted suggestion to expand usage. Alternatively, if the user account doesn't have a certain number of clients, or if site traffic is too low, a different email gets sent, to encourage users to further their engagement and activate.

3. **Trial extension on Day 16**: If a user has shown that they intend to use the product, they receive a personal email with the option to extend the free trial two days after its expiry. This is a simple email that provides an opportunity to win back users who may not have had time to evaluate the product.

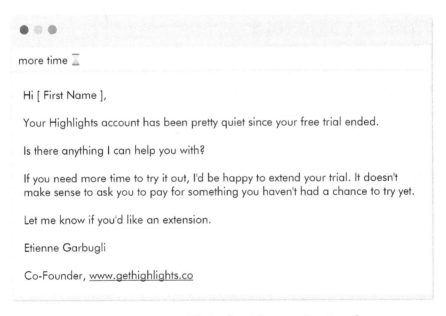

Figure 42.4 – Highlights' Trial Extension Email

Spend time analyzing cohorts in depth. Understand key breakpoints. Evaluate if it is relevant to use email or In-App messages to help influence behaviors. Quantify the impact when possible. Sometimes you can create a business case to justify *productizing* certain fixes.

Keep track of the issues. Sometimes it will be easier to address the product, and sometimes it won't.

Lifecycle emails can be really helpful for support, but also for behavior reinforcement.

If your time is getting consumed by repetitive tasks, consider turning to email automation.

Look for bigger wins, and grow performance with lifecycle emails.

It's important to remember that, as entrepreneur Patrick McKenzie says[101], lifecycle emails are meant to be temporary:

"The end goal of lifecycle emails is to eventually not need them, in the same way that you don't permanently install training wheels. To accomplish this, lifecycle emails should be set up to nudge people along through the most critical inflection points of the journey from signup to thriving user. They're kind of like a joint between two bones, in that sense: acting as the connective tissue that links one key activity to the next."

43

Upgrade, Upsell & Expansion Revenue Sequences

A really good conversion rate for free-to-paid freemium products is 4%. That's the conversion rate achieved by Dropbox and Evernote, while best-in-class products like Spotify get over 26%[102].

Now let me tell you how we managed to get up to 42% of weekly subscriptions from email and In-App messages at LANDR. As a transactional freemium product, LANDR had a really good conversion rate. On top of its subscription model, users were able to purchase individual masterings as one-off transactions.

The user base had a strong willingness to buy, but there was a degree of complexity associated with determining the optimal path for conversion. *Which plans do we promote? When do we promote subscriptions? How do we do it?*

One of the key analyses we were running at the time was revenue cohorts per month for all signup cohorts. We would do breakdowns by monthly signup cohorts and revenue per month.

Through this analysis, the team could quickly answer questions like *'how much money did we generate in the past month from people that signed up 19 months ago?'* We could compare the monetization of different cohorts over time, and re-evaluate progress month after month. It was an easy way to understand consumption patterns.

Here's an example of the data we were looking at:

Segment	Signups	Month 1	Month 2	Month 3	Month 4	Month 5	Month 6
Month 1	7,500	$25,000	$13,500	$7,500	$6,300	$6,200	$6,600
Month 2	7,800	$31,000	$16,500	$8,800	$7,600	$7,400	
Month 3	8,100	$29,500	$17,500	$9,200	$8,100		
Month 4	8,400	$32,000	$18,800	$9,600			
Month 5	8,900	$33,500	$20,100				
Month 6	9,400	$36,000					

Month 1	Month 2	Month 3	Month 4	Month 5	Month 6
$3.33	$1.80	$1.00	$0.84	$0.83	$0.88
$3.97	$2.12	$1.13	$0.97	$0.95	
$3.64	$2.16	$1.14	$1.00		
$3.81	$2.24	$1.14			
$3.76	$2.26				
$3.83					

Figure 43.1 – Revenue Cohorts Per Month Example

As a business with a freemium model, there was really no reason why we couldn't monetize the 20+ monthly cohorts already signed up to use the product.

It turns out that probabilities were also on our side. According to the book *Marketing Metrics*, the likelihood of selling to an existing customer is 60–70%, while the likelihood of selling to a new prospect is only 5–20%[103].

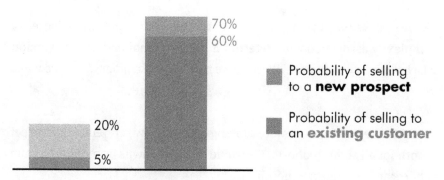

Figure 43.2 – Sales Probability Comparison

Thinking through this challenge made us come at it from a different angle.

We first set up an upgrade email at the 14-day mark. To maximize conversions, we set up reminders a little later for the users that decided not to upgrade. We also added upsell emails for users that had churned in the past, depending on their cancellation reasons.

Once those campaigns were in place, we began work on a much more elaborate upsell program to monetize past cohorts. We set out to identify the behaviors that often lead to subscription purchases:

- *Are the people mastering five times a week more likely to upgrade?*
- *Are the people who use this or that feature more likely to upgrade?*
- *Do the people who use this file format upgrade?*

Looking at the data, we identified dozens of segmentation patterns worth targeting for upsells. We added each and every one of those to our experiment board.

To minimize the *unknown* variables, and test the various patterns, we used proven upsell email copy based on what was already working in other parts of our program.

We sent upsell emails to samples of 500–1,000 users that matched the patterns, and launched experiment after experiment.

If a test worked, we improved the email and adapted the copy to the specific context. If it didn't, we just moved on to the next experiment.

This testing process helped us learn a lot about purchase behaviors, offers, copy, and the discounts that encouraged users to upgrade.

But because the patterns were mostly random, we started running into overlap issues. As summer rolled around, send volumes slowed down, and so did sales. We came to the realization that behavioral targeting—by picking behavior patterns—wouldn't allow us to scale the program.

We eventually reworked the entire upsell program around the concept of train tracks introduced in Chapter #5.

Freemium users now had their own train tracks. They received different upsell emails every few months. Between each attempt, we built up their perception of the product value. Each upsell email users received was based on their actual behavior. Every week the upsell program converted users across 20+ monthly cohorts. Sales and performance increased, and soon enough, ARPU per cohort was growing.

To cap it off, we also used transactional emails to promote subscriptions:

"You just mastered [X] tracks. You can get unlimited mastering at a better quality for just the cost of [Y]."

Monetization is key in SaaS. It's a way to confirm that your product is valued and valuable. And it's a way to fund business growth.

To successfully upsell users, you have to find the right time to sell a subscription and make an appropriate ask.

'*Right*' and '*Appropriate*' are the key words there.

Whether your product has a free trial or you're using a freemium model, it's important to set up an upgrade email. Many businesses don't do this, and it hurts their conversion rate.

It's an easy win. Some people will upgrade just because you ask. With the number of free products on the market, it's possible that some users never realized that your product had premium functionalities they could benefit from.

Zapier's upgrade email is a good example of this:

● ○ ●

Your Trial Ends Tomorrow

Hey [First Name], Wade here,

Your free 14-day trial of Zapier's premium services ends tomorrow (Oct 24, 2019 at 6:31 p.m. CST). That means you'll no longer have access to Zaps with multiple steps, Premium Apps (like Salesforce, Zendesk, PayPal, and others), or other paid features.

Once your trial ends, though, you'll be switched to the Zapier Free Plan. It comes with 5 Zaps, 100 monthly Tasks, and updates every 15 minutes.

Any workflows you have that don't meet your plan's limits will be turned off. But if you want to build automations with multiple steps or use other premium features, you can upgrade to a Premium Plan.

Learn More About Premium Plans

Thanks for trying Zapier!

Wade Foster
Co-Founder & CEO of Zapier

P.S. If you didn't get enough time to try Zapier over the past two weeks, simply reply to this email to let me know and we can extend your trial.

Figure 43.3 – Zapier's Upgrade Email

Like Zapier, you can use loss aversion[104] to your advantage. People are inherently afraid of losing something they already have. If there's a sense of ownership, you can make users want to "Get the features back". If the users are engaged, a simple email should be enough.

To make your email successful, suggest the appropriate subscription based on a user's needs or usage.

Many businesses try to maximize revenue by constantly promoting their most expensive plans, but it is usually more effective to offer the best plan for a given user's needs. A more expensive plan can lead to frustration, and drive users to churn if they realize that they are paying for functionalities they don't need.

Alternatively, if it's not possible to promote a plan based on a user's engagement and feature use, offer your most popular plan.

Some users will buy, others won't.

Stop upselling once users subscribe. Add them to your Retention sequences, or the most appropriate train tracks based on your program.

Re-establish your product's value for non-buyers. *Are they still using your product?* Work on overcoming any objections, show more (or different) product value, try again to upsell them using a different angle.

Different types of users will respond to different types of pitches. These might include:

- quantification of value (e.g. you'll save $700 per year);
- a hard push;
- discounts; or
- case studies (etc).

FreshBooks, creator of a popular invoice and accounting product, tries a few different approaches during its trials.

● ● ●

Find the perfect plan for your business

You have 16 days left in
your trial. Upgrade Now

Hey there,

How's your free trial going? With just 16 days left, you're already halfway through.
Do your future self a favor and upgrade now so you can continue using Fresh
Books uninterrupted. Plans start at just $15 and come packed with features to help
you get paid faster. Plus, don't start paying until your 30-day trial is over.

Lite
$15 per month USD

- Bill up to 5 active clients
- Unlimited Invoices & Estimates
- Track Time & Expenses
- Accept Online Payments

Select →

Plus
$25 per month USD

- Bill up to 50 active clients
- All Lite Features
- Automatic Payment Reminders
- Schedule Recurring Invoices
- Send Proposals

Select →

Premium
$50 per month USD

- Bill up to 500 active clients
- All Lite Features
- All Plus Features

Select →

Not sure which plan is the right fit for your business? I'm happy to help. Give me
(or any one of my colleagues) a call at 1-866-303-6061 or send an email.

Until next time,

Rachel Guloien
Support Rockstar

Figure 43.4 – FreshBooks' Upgrade Email 1

189

Have You Seen the Difference FreshBooks Makes?

 cloud accounting

You have 9 days left in your trial. Upgrade Now

FreshBooks + You = Success

You have 9 days left to explore, but we hope you're already convinced. With FreshBooks in your corner you'll:

✓ **Quickly send professional-looking invoices**

✓ **Keep accurate expense records for tax time**

✓ **Get paid faster by accepting credit cards**

So, what do you say? Ready to do this?

Select a Plan

Still need time to try everything out? No need to stress, there are still 9 days left on your trial. Plus, there are handy resources like the Learning Hub, FAQs and FreshBooks Support Team that can help you make the most of the rest of your trial.

 Have a Question?
Give the FreshBooks Support Team a call at 1-866-303-6061 or send an email.

Figure 43.5 – FreshBooks' Upgrade Email 2

You Have 4 Days Left on Your Trial

There are 4 days
left before your trial ends
<u>Upgrade Now</u>

Your Future Self Will Thank You
Upgrade Today and Get 35% Off for 3 Months*

Real talk: Many small businesses fail. Be the exception. From professional invoices to automatic expense tracking, FreshBooks offers you the tools that will set you up for success.

The Decision Is Yours: Are You Ready to Thrive?

To make it even easier to make the right choice, FreshBooks is giving you **35% off for 3 months** when you upgrade today. With **plans starting at just $9.75,** there's no better time.

> Upgrade Now

The best part? You don't start paying until your trial is over. Your future self will thank you.

Need a Hand Picking a Plan?
Give the FreshBooks Support Team a call at <u>1-866-303-6061</u> or <u>send an email.</u>

Figure 43.6 – FreshBooks' Upgrade Email 3

There's a lot to learn from their upgrade sequence.

Beyond the initial upgrade and the value expansion emails, you should create upsells across your different signup cohorts.

As we did at LANDR, you need to look for signals that indicate users are getting value from the product. These may include:

- quick activation
- frequent use
- high NPS scores (proven to be highly-correlated to expansion revenue[105])
- recent product use
- frequent use of *metered* features like your product's value metric
- frequent visits to pricing or payment pages
- high engagement on emails and communications
- feature requests
- consistent use
- positive word of mouth
- usage after cancellation of a subscription
- use of premium features during the trial

Such signals can help you to understand who within your user base may be more likely to upgrade. Once you have identified some clear signals, you can start creating a program, for example:

- Day 122: Upsell attempt
- Day 182: Upsell attempt (+60)
- Day 242: Upsell attempt (+60)
- Day 302: Upsell attempt (+60), and so on

To avoid overlaps, and ensure you attempt to upsell all of your users, you should select key dates and send the appropriate upsell emails based on past actions. Change the pitches, approach messaging from different angles, and evaluate performance.

One of the biggest mistakes most new email marketers make is to send three or four sales emails back-to-back. You should be selling, at most, 20% of the time. So, make sure you balance user and business value.

You'll have to test with your audience, but sometimes all users need is a nudge. You can use transactional emails to nudge your users. Summary emails, *loop* emails, or even transactions receipts can be used to promote subscription plans. Highlight key benefits, and find ways to demonstrate them when possible.

Zapier warns free users when they reach 80% capacity on a metered metric, part of their paid subscription plans. It's a simple reminder, and allows them to drive users to upgrade without having to offer any kind of discount.

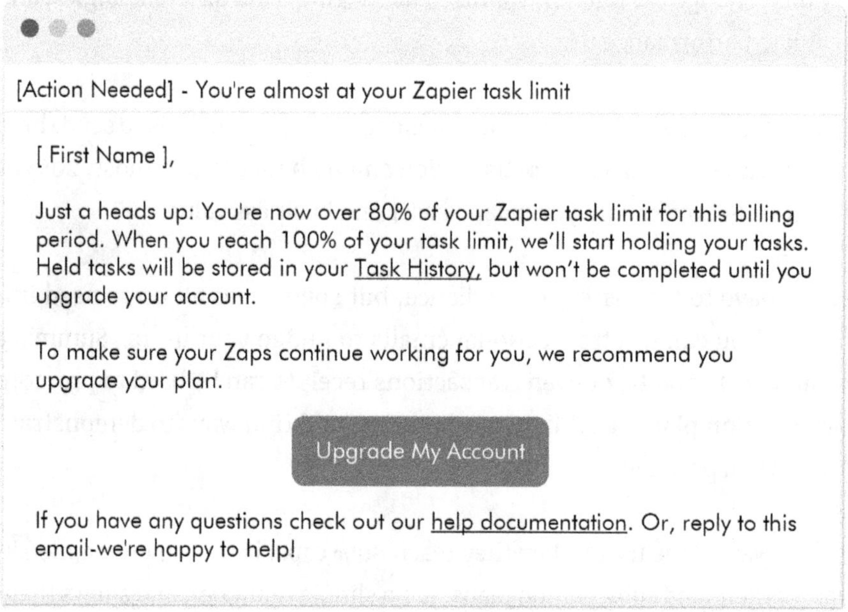

[Action Needed] - You're almost at your Zapier task limit

[First Name],

Just a heads up: You're now over 80% of your Zapier task limit for this billing period. When you reach 100% of your task limit, we'll start holding your tasks. Held tasks will be stored in your Task History, but won't be completed until you upgrade your account.

To make sure your Zaps continue working for you, we recommend you upgrade your plan.

Upgrade My Account

If you have any questions check out our help documentation. Or, reply to this email-we're happy to help!

Figure 43.7 – Zapier's Freemium Upsell Email

A few things to consider with upgrade and upsell emails:

- **Product first**: If your product sucks and you're unable to get conversions, upgrade emails won't magically drive sales. You need to improve your product first.
- **Contextual is better**: Email is one extra step removed from the conversion. If users spend a lot of time in your app and the product context can help drive conversions, in-product upsells will work best. Your users will be closer to the finish line. You can use In-App messages, popups, or in-product callouts to drive sales. The more contextual the better.
- **Show the value**: You can use CTAs that communicate the main benefits of your app, testimonies from customers showcasing the product's value, or contrast the outcomes of upgrading vs not upgrading. There are lots of ways to get customers to upgrade. Think through different scenarios.
- **Don't devalue your product**: Discounts and offers can be used as

justification for sending upsell emails. Over time, however, discounts will hurt your retention and ability to monetize your product. For this reason, you need to be strategic with discounts to avoid *devaluing* your subscription plans[106]. Make users *earn* their discounts. Use them sparingly to get users over the finish line.

- **Right time, right discounts**: If you decide to use discounts, 10–20% tends to be the minimum to get users to act. Unless your product is really expensive, discounts of less than 10% won't be enough to get users to convert. You should use 30% for special sales, and 40–50% only for customers who have already bought like churners, or for the rare or exclusive promos. In general, users who *need* a discount to upgrade are often the wrong customers to start with.

- **Testing upsells is easy**: Upsells are fairly straightforward to test. You have a clear goal (i.e. a purchase), you can monitor revenue and conversion rates, and you can run A/B tests based on your messaging and the offer you choose.

Start with a basic upgrade email. Follow it up with upsell emails. Evaluate adding upgrade CTAs in transactional emails. Expand from there to grow your revenue.

Your upgrade email will be key. Refine it before expanding your program too far.

Don't expect a single campaign to drive all your revenue. The *combined* performance of different campaigns is what generates predictable revenue.

Start mapping your customer journeys and the paths to upgrades. You can push Upgrade, Upsell & Expansion Revenue sequences really far—as we clearly did.

44

Retention Sequences

A lot of SaaS businesses focus on acquisition and monetization. One grows the user base, while the other grows the coffers. With more revenue, you can spend more on ads, branding, and acquisition. You can also grow your team. But the metric that kills SaaS businesses more often than any other is retention—your ability to get re-purchases and consistently grow customer lifetime value. With better retention you get more revenue per user, build predictability, and you can spend more on acquisition knowing that you're building on solid unit economics[107].

Good retention signals customer health, product stickiness, competitive differentiation, and pricing power.

In SaaS, cancellations or churn negates growth. You may be able to close $10,000 of new bookings each month, but if your monthly revenue churn, the dollar amount of canceled or churned customers, is also $10,000, your business isn't growing.

Another way to look at it is that if you start the year with 100 customers and lose 5% of your customers each month (i.e. 5% monthly churn), then your business loses 46 customers during the year (i.e. annual churn rate of 46%). To grow just by one customer, you will need to sign up at least 47 new customers during the year. This will be really difficult to overcome.

According to investor David Skok[108], best-in-class churn rates hover around 5-7% annually; that's about one customer out of 200 per month. Depending on your product and your market, it's possible to get there, and email can be a major driver of retention.

So, how do you improve retention?

The best way to improve retention is through your product, by focusing on how it delivers and communicates value to your customers. Your product is the core thing your users pay for.

Email, text messages, and push notifications rely on user attention, opens, reads, and clicks. Because of this, they are more *indirect* ways to influence user behaviors. Whereas, initially at least, your product *has* your users' attention.

With retention, your goal is to improve the retention curve.

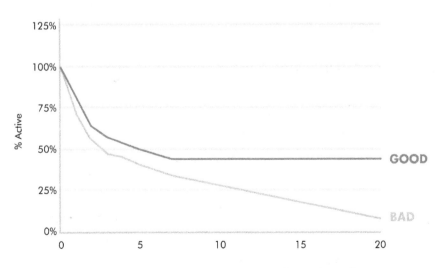

Figure 44.1 – Retention Curve Flattening

As growth expert Brian Balfour says[109]: "The important thing is that it (the retention curve) flattens."

Email and other communications are *part* of your service. They can have a big impact on churn and the customer lifetime, especially when used in conjunction with *valued* product improvements.

To use email to reduce churn, you first need to understand the kind of product you are dealing with.

Is your product naturally used:

- every day?
- once a week?
- once a month?
- every now and then (episodic)?

Episodic products like SurveyMonkey or LANDR—where music mastering has traditionally been associated with album releases every year or every other year—are not *natural* fits for subscription businesses. Inconsistent usage patterns make these businesses better candidates for on-demand or transactional revenue models like one-off sales. This doesn't mean that subscriptions can't work for these businesses, it just means that retention will be more challenging.

Understanding the usage cycle of your product helps set realistic expectations for product engagement. This, in turn, helps you understand the kind of email program you should be running, and how much *pushing* will be required.

If your product has natural daily engagement, you might not need to send a lot of emails to improve retention. But if people use your product every year or every three months, then monthly subscriptions will be hard to pull off.

Would you expect to buy tax preparation software as a subscription? Probably not.

Beyond onboarding—the element of your product that has the greatest impact on retention—there are both direct and indirect ways to improve retention.

1. Annual Subscriptions

The easiest, and the most direct way to improve retention is to increase the percentage of annual subscribers. More annual subscribers means more cash up-front, and a higher customer lifetime value (CLV).

A few ways to do that include:

- **Defaulting your subscription plans to annual**—at LANDR, this alone increased the share of yearly plans and weekly subscription revenue.
- **Offering additional (and valued) benefits exclusively on yearly plans**—it can be a good idea to incentivize annual upgrades. Discounts can work, but extra features and benefits can often work even better.
- **Offering engaged monthly subscribers to switch to an annual subscription**—or, if that's too big a jump, you can create quarterly or bi-annual subscription plans.

Customers on monthly subscriptions have 12 decision points when they may decide to cancel each year. That means they get 12 invoices—that's 12 reminders to cancel. If they are getting value, bumping them to annual subscriptions makes a ton of sense.

At LANDR, we had a lot of success using levers. For example: "You already paid 30% of a yearly subscription, if you upgrade to a yearly plan today, we'll give you 30% off a yearly subscription."

With engaged monthly subscribers, you may not even need a discount.

Podia simply positions it as "Get two months free" which, as email marketer Christoph Engelhardt points out, converts 20% better than advertising the equivalent discount of 17%[110].

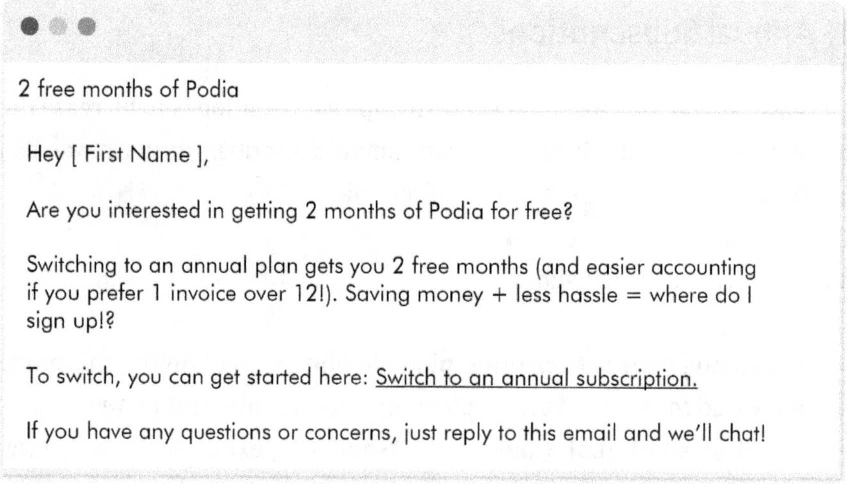

● ● ●

2 free months of Podia

Hey [First Name],

Are you interested in getting 2 months of Podia for free?

Switching to an annual plan gets you 2 free months (and easier accounting if you prefer 1 invoice over 12!). Saving money + less hassle = where do I sign up!?

To switch, you can get started here: Switch to an annual subscription.

If you have any questions or concerns, just reply to this email and we'll chat!

Figure 44.2 – Podia's Upsell Email

In this case, Podia also points out that annual subscriptions help simplify accounting (extra benefit!).

For this type of campaign, you need to make the conversion path as quick and direct as possible. Provide an easy, one-click way to switch to annual billing if you can. The increase in conversion rate will be well worth the investment.

2. Credit Card & Payment Churn

In SaaS, 20–40% of churn will often be "delinquent", or credit card and payment churn[111].

There are more than 130 different reasons why credit cards fail beyond card expiry. As your business grows, it will be very difficult for your team to keep on top of all failure reasons.

You can increase retention by bringing down your credit card failure rate. Paid services like Churn Buster[112] or ProfitWell Retain[113] can help you do this. But using these services often means adding a new vendor to your setup, which may not be a good idea.

If you can funnel up key payment issues to your email marketing platform, which is sometimes complex, then you can set up dunning or payment failure emails to help correct key scenarios: failed payments, expiring credit cards, insufficient funds, etc.

When these scenarios arise, it's often best to stop your other email campaigns and the user's subscription to catch their attention.

This will require some development, but 20–40% of churners can be a lot of subscribers. Worse, only about 5% of delinquent churners ever re-subscribe after the payment churn[114].

3. Value Communication

You can also improve retention by reminding your users of the value that they are *already* getting from your product. A great way to do this is through transactional emails—the emails most businesses tend to neglect.

Good candidates include:

- success emails
- key "loop" emails
- reports/summaries

At LANDR, we were sending download emails whenever someone mastered a song. This meant hundreds of thousands of emails each week. It was a major opportunity to remind subscribers of the unique value they were getting from the service, by highlighting the key improvements LANDR made to their music.

If you don't have a similar *loop* email, you can create one. For example, LinkedIn uses work anniversaries to leverage a completely made up concept for engagement purposes. And it has worked for them.

Are there ways your team could create a similar "loop" email?

A great example of report emails comes from TextExpander, a productivity app I use.

Your Monthly TextExpander Report

Hi [First Name],

Payment Reminder:

This is just a friendly reminder that your annual billing is coming up in the next **30 days.**

Here's how you've been doing with TextExpander in the last month:

787
snippets expanded

1h 26m
saved

Doing well, keep it up!

Here are a few resources to give you some ideas for even more snippets. Check out our Public Groups for other ready-made snippet groups you can use.

We have lots of ideas for new snippets in our Tips center.

Check out our **Public Groups** for other ready-made snippet groups you can use.

TextExpander is chock full of neat features to help automate your typing floW, our **Videos** can tell you more.

We have lots of ideas for new snippets in our **Tips center.**

Figure 44.3 – TextExpander's Summary Email

Every month, they give me information I don't have. At a quick glance, I can assess that the product is well worth the $40 I spend on my subscription each year.

For B2B products, report emails are typically more about showing the value of the product to colleagues or managers than understanding it ourselves. They are what entrepreneur Patrick McKenzie calls the "Get Promoted" email[115].

4. Feature Launches

As noted in a study by ProfitWell[116], the elements that most influence Net Promoter Scores are:

1. brand;
2. support; and
3. the speed at which new features are shipped.

As the buyer for several analytics and email products at Highlights and LANDR, I can vouch for that.

When a product is missing a feature that you are hoping the vendor will add, and you feel that the company is constantly shipping new features, you don't *need* to think about switching products. You can simply expect that eventually they will address your feature request.

Feature launch emails can help by 1) demonstrating momentum, and 2) showcasing new or different value in the product.

The important thing is to create a cadence, a rhythmic sequence that communicates improvements every week, every month, or every quarter.

Of course, you shouldn't broadcast every single feature to every subscriber. Segmentation is a key part of communicating valued product improvements.

Intercom shared the following framework for feature and product launches in their book, *Intercom on Product Management*[117]:

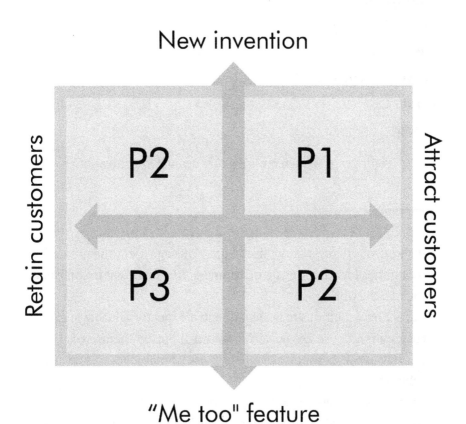

Figure 44.4 – Intercom's Feature Groupings

	P1	P2	P3	P4
Changes page	✓	✓	✓	✓
In-App messages	✓	✓	✓	
Landing page	✓	✓		
Press coverage	✓	✓		
Email	✓	✓		
Video	✓			

Figure 44.5 – Intercom's Feature Launch Prioritization

In their model:

- P1s are your biggest announcements. These present the greatest opportunities for attracting new customers. It's important to shout about them to the world.
- P2s are new solutions to problems, and are mostly valuable to existing customers. These are powerful features, but by themselves they're unlikely to persuade new customers to use your product over an existing solution.
- P3s are the improvements that you ship to fill gaps in a product, or simply to improve it. Existing customers have likely been asking for them. In these cases, it's a good idea to focus on updating the users who were asking for these features.

Come up with your own strategy. You should create a cadence by organizing feature launches around your P1 and P2 features. A launch per month can help create a sense of momentum.

Tell a story with every update. Position the value to your subscribers.

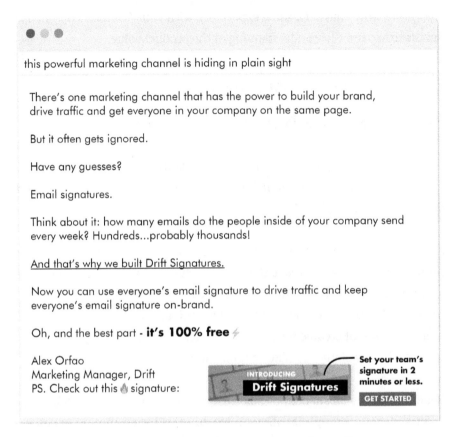

Figure 44.6 – Drift's Feature Launch Email

An alternative approach is to promote features your users *aren't* already using, but would most likely find valuable.

Constant new discoveries can have the same effect on your subscribers—you are unlocking new superpowers for them:

"Wow, I didn't know [Product] did that."

For this reason, I'm a big fan of automating launch emails beyond the original launch date.

New users won't have the same experience with your product. You can use emails to expand their understanding of the product value.

5. Extra Content & Communications

To further improve retention, think beyond your product.

How else can you help your users achieve their desired outcomes? What else do they value? Content? Entertainment? Networking opportunities? Discounts on other products? Swag?

At LANDR, because the product had few features, we often had to focus on promoting the benefits *around* the product (the community, the advice, the support, etc). We created LANDR Select, the premium subscriber newsletter, to expand the perceived value of the subscription. This newsletter featured premium content created for the exclusive use of subscribers. Our goal was to make the newsletter *feel* like a product unboxing[118].

Benefits come in all shapes and sizes. You can expand value by giving away additional services, special offers, opportunities for promotion or collaboration, exclusive content or information, access to private communities, invitations to select events, etc.

Mapping the lifecycles of your customers' subscriptions should allow you to find ways to increase their perceptions of value. Your emails can then build on that value.

6. Product Communications

Email is just *one* way to connect with your customers. There are lots of other *channels* you can use to help reinforce the value of your product: pre-loaders, coachmarks, chat, pop-ups, walk-throughs, notifications, SMS messages, In-App messages, and so on.

Switching up the channels can help keep the messaging fresh and interesting.

Each channel has its pros and cons. The ideal retention program will have the product, In-App messages, and emails all working hand-in-hand.

Think holistically, and use:

- transactional emails
- pre-loaders
- success messages
- support follow-ups
- FAQs
- customer success reach-outs
- or any method of communication really

There's always an opportunity to communicate the value that your subscribers are getting from your product if you are looking for it. Get creative.

A few things to consider as you're putting together your retention sequence:

- **Retention is notoriously hard to experiment with**: The evaluation cycle for any test you run will take at least a month (i.e. monthly subscriptions), but could take much longer if you're looking for statistical significance.
- **Attribution will be difficult**: It won't be easy to attribute the impact of specific experiments or communications on retention. *Did your onboarding email improve retention, or the customer success team did?*
- **Focus on email opens**: You will have a hard time assessing the impact of product, support, and emails on retention. Focus almost exclusively on the customers that open and interact with your communications. For example, of all the new customers that opened your first onboarding email, *how many completed all the onboarding steps within 7 days? 14 days? 30 days?*

Perception of value tends to decrease over time. To improve retention, you must constantly remind your customers of the value that your product provides. This is true for both monthly and yearly subscriptions. Don't wait until the end of the year to reengage your yearly subscribers—it might be too late by then!

A dirty secret in SaaS is non-consumption. Lots of products have zombie customers[119], customers that pay, but don't actually use the product. This is one of the reasons why products like Spendesk, which are designed to track subscriptions across organizations, are gaining traction.

You could decide to warn users of impending payments, but this can often lead to cancellations. While this is a *fairer* way to build your business, it can have negative impacts. I've heard both sides of the argument.

No matter what you decide to do, you should avoid chargebacks. Chargebacks can lead to extra fees and damage your business's credit score.

As growth expert Sean Ellis says[120], in SaaS, value delivery drives sustainable growth.

You have to focus on creating value, and then on communicating that value.

Start with annual and dunning emails. Look for *loops* and automations to improve value communication. Expand from there.

45

Referral Sequences

A good NPS sequence can help you capture and leverage user feedback, get reviews, and drive fresh acquisition at the top of the funnel.

Your NPS sequence will be based on the Net Promoter Score®, a management tool designed to gauge customer loyalty that was developed in 1993 by Frederick Reichheld, and popularized in part by Harvard.

Net Promoter Score surveys are now standard in over two thirds of Fortune 1000 companies[121]. The NPS is in no way a perfect measure[122], but it has been shown to correlate to satisfaction and loyalty[123].

Part of the reason why the NPS got adopted so widely is because of how easy it is to collect and analyze survey responses.

You are almost certainly familiar with the survey's main question:

"On a scale of 0 to 10, how likely are you to recommend our [Business/Product/Service] to a friend or colleague?"

When running NPS surveys, it's generally a good idea to ask a follow-up question to capture the respondent's reasoning:

"What is the primary reason for your score?"

At LANDR a few years back, we built a backend system to create surveys. The idea was to be able to integrate the NPS—or any other survey really—directly into the body of emails, or in In-App messages. Then users would click links, and their answers would get sent to our database. For NPS specifically, the system propagated the answers to our email platform, Intercom, and also calculated the scores for reporting. The results were great, but it was an extremely complex solution.

I really wouldn't recommended doing this today.

In all likelihood, your referral sequence will be sent in parallel with and on top of your retention sequence. Your goal will be to take different snapshots over the course of subscribers' lifetimes and assess their loyalty.

To get started with your sequence, look at the key stages and try to target the biggest drops in churn.

You should start during the first month of subscription—three weeks in—so that you can follow up and recover if subscribers' NPS scores are lower than anticipated.

Here's what the schedule could look like if you intend to send regular check-ins:

- Day 23: NPS survey
- Day 26: NPS follow-up (+3)
- Day 76: NPS survey (+50)
- Day 168: NPS survey(+92)
- Day 231: NPS survey (+63), etc

At LANDR, we sent surveys in months one, three, six, and eight.

Especially in the first month, it can be a good idea to send a reminder 2–3 days after the first email if users haven't opened, or responded to the survey.

In SaaS, Net Promoter Score surveys are about action, not just measurement.

Through the survey, you'll collect a range of scores:

- **0 to 6**: Detractors, *likely* to churn
- **7 or 8**: Passives, who don't really care or not care about your product
- **9 or 10**: Promoters, advocates or fans who may be willing to refer your product to others

You can view these scores as inputs for follow-up questions and email sequences. Each score can be handled differently, for example you can ask Detractors *"What is the primary reason for your score?"*

With Passives, you can ask *"What can we do to improve?"* or *"What is the one thing we could do to make you happier?"*

Questions you can ask Promoters might be *"Which [Feature/Benefit] do you value/use the most?"* or *"What do you feel is the biggest benefit you've received from [Product]?"*

Detractors and Passives can also be good candidates for interviews to help you learn how to improve the product.

Based on the insights gleaned from the follow-up answers, you can learn how to improve the experience, and then follow up with appropriate email sequences.

In general, you'll want to *woo* Passives, *win over* Detractors, and *maximize the contribution of* Promoters.

This can be done by:

1. **Asking for reviews** on G2Crowd, GetApp, Capterra, Google, Trustpilot, or any other relevant sites in your industry. Or ask for testimonies, endorsements, or case studies in B2B.
2. **Asking for direct referrals**, be it a shout-out on social media, inviting friends or colleagues to use the product, or giving promotional links that help your users make affiliate income.

Airbnb notoriously created a very successful two-sided referral program based on the promise that both parties—the referrer and the invitee—would make money[124]. We tried doing that specifically at LANDR, but didn't have much success.

For this type of approach to work:

- your users need to have their own audiences; and
- they must be motivated by the idea of making more money.

This is not always the case.

According to a Nielsen study, 92% of consumers trust a recommendation from people they know[125].

The beauty with referrals is that they can have a compounding effect by bringing in new users not naturally connected to your user base. Setting up a referral sequence is a lot easier than it once was. Marketing automation platforms, for example Autopilot, Drip, HubSpot, Intercom, and Marketo, have built-in functionalities designed to capture NPS survey responses.

Alternatively, there are Net Promoter Score survey tools like Wootric[126], Delighted[127], Promoter.io[128], AskNicely[129], or Survicate[130], which can integrate with or be used in parallel of your email marketing platform. Many of these tools will allow you to generate complete reports and send responses to Slack or other group chats. Your business's NPS score—a range from -100 to +100—has to be calculated in a special way. There are free calculators online that you can use to run the numbers[131].

So, *what should the flow be?*

If most of your subscribers use your product daily or weekly, you can decide to run your NPS survey via an In-App message.

If the usage is weekly or monthly, or a large portion of your subscribers are not overly engaged, email will be better.

Surveys via In-App messages will be faster, more direct, and allow you to get a higher completion rate. Email will allow you to reach users off-site.

Alternatively, you could set automation rules to decide who gets an In-App message, and who gets an email. In this case, you need to make sure users are removed from your NPS follow-up sequences once they have filled out a survey.

If you are in B2B, it can be a good idea to ask both end users (the people using the product the most frequently) and account owners (the people managing the account). Their different perspectives will help you understand internal dynamics and adapt your communications accordingly.

Get started with setting up your first message. Test different subject lines. Since the email content will always feature the same survey, and you don't want to bore your users, it's a good idea to switch up your subject lines between the different probes.

Here are a few subject lines you can test:

- "Tell us how we're doing"
- "[First Name] do you have a moment?"
- "How are we doing?"
- "Help us read your mind about [Product]"
- "I have a serious question for you..."
- "Help us improve [Product] by taking this survey"
- "[First Name], help us make [Product] better!"
- "quick question"
- "I need your feedback!"

Keep your email straight to the point with big click zones to lower the friction for your users.

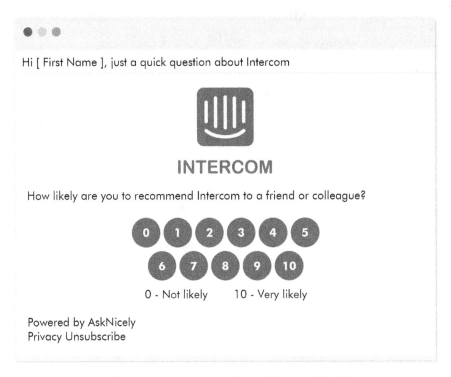

Figure 45.1 – Intercom's NPS Survey Email

Reach out to all your subscribers on the 23rd day of their subscription. Follow up with the same email with a different subject line 2–3 days after if you don't get a response.

Keep an eye out for low scores. You can have customer success reach out to these users for recovery.

One problem you'll notice is that a lot of your most disengaged subscribers just won't respond. This can be a telltale sign and can help you anticipate churn.

Moving forward, you can use similar signals to create a customer health score[132] and identify subscribers at risk of canceling.

Depending on which platform you use, you could set up a survey follow-up and thank you directly through the platform. Otherwise it can be a bit trickier to track and manage scores, but there are ways around it, for example by using Zapier[133].

The ability to store and match data with the appropriate user profiles will be important. Make sure that this can be done.

For Detractors and Passives you can begin doing value expansion, an extension of onboarding as we have seen in the Welcome & Onboarding deep dive.

For Promoters, you can promote a referral program like Podia's.

Earn 💰 for referring creators to Podia

Hi [First Name],

Our number one goal at Podia is to help creators like you earn money.

You already know about our online selling platform, but today, I want to share another way that we do that.

It's called the Refer-a-Creator program, and it pays you 💰💰💰 for referring your friends to Podia.

You'll earn a 30% commission every month that your referred creator stays with us.

That means if you send us a creator who pays $79/month, you'll earn $26.30 every month!

You can see how referring a few creators begins to add up pretty quickly

Here's what Becky Mollenkamp, a Podia customer and one of our Refer-a-Creator partners, says about the program:

"I love being an affiliate for Podia. The program is incredibly generous and simple to use and understand. Podia's customer service is always top-notch, and the same holds true with how well they treat their affiliates."

Signing up to become a Refer-a-Creator partner is easy. Just click here to get started.

If you have any questions at all, reply to this email and let me know 😃

Cheers,
Len

Figure 45.2 – Podia's Referral Program Email

Alternatively, you could ask for product reviews, or friend invitations. It can be a good idea to alternate the ask over time so that you maximize the contribution of Promoters.

It's also a good idea to monitor gaps in ratings via analytics, your NPS survey system, or perhaps even the segments you have created in your email marketing platform.

If your product is freemium, you may also want to survey engaged freemium users. Asking them for referrals can allow you to extract more value from your free tier. This is one of the main ways in which products like Zoom and Slack have grown over the years.

The Referral sequence will help to feed your referral engine and capture actionable feedback for your business. It can also help to create a better customer experience and to compound your business's growth.

It's definitely a must.

46

Reactivation Sequences

Unfortunately, even with the best email program, not all users and customers will stick around.

With the average free-to-paid conversion rate hovering at around 4%[134], it's actually quite likely that, over time, your user base will start being overtaken by disengaged users. Maybe these users didn't have a need, maybe you failed to efficiently communicate product value, maybe they have found another solution, or maybe they just forgot about your product. No matter the reason, it's 6–8 times cheaper to retain existing users and customers than to acquire new ones[135].

According to Kissmetrics, the average list's inactive rate is around 60%[136]. After analyzing six billion emails, MailChimp concluded that, on average, 7% of overall business revenue comes from inactive users[137].

Once other major sequences (onboarding, upgrade, retention, and referral) have been covered, and 30% or more of your users have become disengaged, it makes sense to start thinking about reactivation sequences.

Should you try to reactivate all past users?

A good metric to evaluate reactivation is your *win-back* rate. You can view this as an activation rate for users who already have an account.

Users weren't necessarily a good fit for your product just because they signed up. The users you want to win back are those that showed *actual interest* in using your product, or at least *should have*.

These might be:

- users who activated
- users who used your product throughout the trial period
- users who were once engaged or active
- users who *demonstrably* got value out of your product
- past paying subscribers
- users who fit your ideal customer profile

We have already covered upsells in the Upgrade, Upsell & Expansion Revenue deep dive, but the reality is that, unless your users have had subscriptions before, they are unlikely to buy cold.

It's a good idea to work on getting them in the product first, and then winning them back *before* attempting to sell them a subscription.

Time is an important dimension when it comes to disengagement, but it isn't the most important. Time may dictate how much your users have missed and how well they remember the product. But interests and desired outcomes will play much bigger roles in convincing users to get back in your product. Your users' goals, interests, or priorities might have changed, but if they are still opening your emails, it's quite likely that the problems your product solves are still on their radar.

You can view the implementation of a reactivation sequence as a series of probes designed to help you understand user disengagement.

The better you are able to connect with your disengaged users' current realities, the more likely you are to spark their interest in giving your product a second chance.

If you're getting started with your reactivation sequence, it could be a good idea to segment your disengaged users by slices of 90 days, that is:

- users who haven't *used* your product in the past 90 days
- users who haven't used your product in the past 91 to 180 days
- users who haven't used your product in the past 181 to 270 days, etc

Users in each segment will have a different experience with your product. Notice the key action here is *used*. The definition of *using* your product should be specific to the way your product gets used.

So, when going through each slice of disengaged users, ask the following questions:

- *What percentage is still engaged with your brand (opens your emails, clicks your ads, writes to support, reads your blog posts, etc)?*
- *Can you infer anything from their behavior? What interests do they have?*
- *Do you have historical data about their goals or interests?*
- *Have you learned anything about their needs since they left?*
- *Is it worth creating further segmentation to address these interests?*

The more closely your segmentation is matched to their interests, the more likely it is that they will want to engage.

To reactivate users, try the following:

1. The Catchup Email

What has changed since these users last used your product?

If you have routinely been making your product more valuable (which you should have been doing), then you should be able to note a few key additions and improvements since they last used your product.

Assess changes for each individual segment. Identify what makes the most sense based on that segment's interests. To be read, your messages need to be relevant.

Speak directly to the users. Create an email that highlights fixes and product updates since they stopped using the product.

These users have the product context, so you can speak to them differently. You want to be very human and tell them clearly how the updates will make them more successful.

If users churned because of the absence of a certain feature, or if they sent feature requests, you can use this information to make the emails feel even more personal. The more personal your email is, the better it will connect.

If you're in B2B, targeting business leads, consider sending these emails manually, and offering up a demo to show the improvements.

The average U.S. smartphone user receives 46 push notifications per day[138]. It's quite likely that a lot of your users have become immune to emails and notifications.

Evaluate your email's win-back performance based on a key action in your product beyond login.

If the goal rate for subscribers opening your emails is more than 5% or 10%, but the open rate is low (10% or less), consider repurposing your email, and targeting users on different channels.

Perhaps you can use SMS messages to engage your subscribers. Or could you engage them on Twitter? Or can you run a re-marketing or retargeting campaign on Facebook, Instagram, AdRoll, or another network? Ad platforms like Facebook allow you to upload email lists to target precise segments of users. Similar campaigns can be very effective.

2. Introducing New Value

In the Retention deep dive we saw that extra content and communications can be used to expand the perception of value. Similar campaigns can also work for reactivation.

Maybe you have created an e-book that can help address one of your users' challenges?

Maybe there's a private community that they can join?

Maybe you can give them a discount on another product they might use?

Think beyond your product. Don't invest too much in creating new benefits or content. Let this strategy prove itself to you, first.

Make it relevant. Keep the messaging simple. The key is to get users back into the product (if possible).

Then you can use product communications like In-App messages to get users to re-engage.

3. Trial Extension Emails

When I was a kid growing up, there was a cable TV station that ran films 24/7. Every year, for a full weekend, they made their service available for free to everyone. Every year, when we found out the date, it became a talking point in school yards—for us it was really a big deal. For a full weekend, we would sit down as a family and watch six or seven *new-ish* movies. It was great!

In spite of the growth in movie downloads over the years, this strategy helped the station to acquire new customers and remain relevant.

They say that an image is worth a thousand words. Well, sometimes trying a product—even one you've already tried before—can be a lot more effective than reading about it.

When users have shown the desire to get value out of a product, you can offer an extended or a premium trial. At this stage, there's very little to lose, so your offer can be very generous.

For example, Help Scout offers to extend their free trial by three times the length of their regular trial[139]:

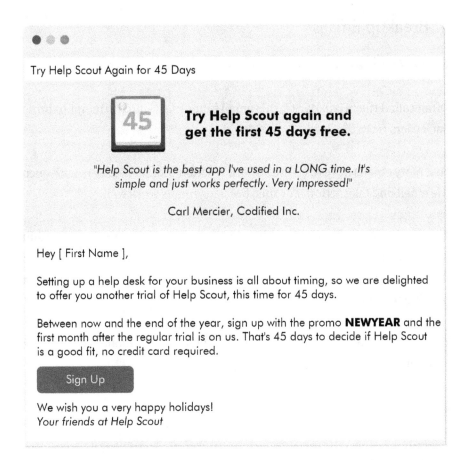

Figure 46.1 – Help Scout's Trial Extension Email

You can use a very straightforward email for this.

Mentioning the offer in the subject line can help to arouse curiosity. It's a good to idea to make this a limited-time offer and to get users to confirm their interest by taking a specific action.

According to Nick Francis, Help Scout's CEO, 10–20% of abandoned trials sign up a second time. Their trial extension email is a big part of their reactivation process.

4. Breakup Emails

Lastly, if all else failed, you can consider sending one last email.

Often called the "Hail Mary", this email is your last-ditch attempt to bring back users from the dead.

Hail Mary emails have to create a shock reaction that makes users both open the email *and* take action. For this, breakup emails work well.

The general idea is to tell users that their account will be terminated within 5, 7, 12, or 14 days unless they sign back in. Keep the email simple and to the point. Make sure the message is clear right from the inbox, without even needing to open the email.

You'll quickly be able to tell which users actually care about keeping their accounts.

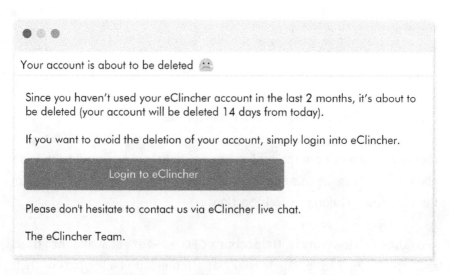

Figure 46.2 – eClincher's Breakup Email

At the end of the grace period, make sure you actually do cancel their accounts. There's really no point in messaging them again if you have already sent all of the emails covered in this chapter.

Test the performance of each email against your win-back rate. As emails start to perform, create a sequence trying to win back users every 20–30 days.

Make sure you remove users from your sequence when you actually do win them back.

Once you have run the full campaign across your entire disengaged user base, consider automating it after a certain number of days of inactivity.

Reactivation is about making your customer lifecycle go full circle. Your business will most likely be in really good shape when you can reliably bring users back from the dead.

Next Steps

Thanks for reading *The SaaS Email Marketing Playbook.*

Unfortunately, reading is one thing, applying is another.

To help you apply the ideas in this book, I have put together a series of templates (interview, reporting, pre-send checklist, etc), examples of successful emails, step-by-step videos, and a subject line pack.

You can download these resources at: **saasplaybook.co/bonus**

Work With Me

Want to take things to the next level? Need more one-on-one help? Looking to expand and accelerate?

Each month, I help half a dozen SaaS companies build, refine, and optimize their email marketing programs. From strategy, to execution, to segmentation, to evaluation, the work helps unlock significant growth for these organizations.

You can learn more about the services or book a call at: **saasplaybook.co/coaching**

Further Reading

Part of my motivation for writing *The SaaS Email Marketing Playbook* comes from the fact that, although there are a lot of resources on email marketing available online, very few have been written from the perspective of subscription businesses.

When we started working on email marketing at LANDR, we had to piece together our own processes and methodologies. This came at the cost of failure, long hours, and exhaustive internet searches.

Fortunately, there are now a lot more resources available on the topic.

To further your understanding of SaaS email marketing, check out the following blogs:

- Appcues (appcues.com)
- Customer-Centric Growth by Lincoln Murphy (sixteenventures.com)
- Fix My Churn (fixmychurn.com)
- Forget the Funnel (forgetthefunnel.com)
- Outfunnel (outfunnel.com)
- SaaS Email Marketing (saasemailmarketing.net)

To dive deeper into the concepts in this book, I recommend reading:

- *Hooked*, Nir Eyal
- *Intercom on Marketing, on Onboarding, on Product Management*, Intercom
- *Lean Analytics*, Alistair Croll and Ben Yoskovitz

- *Lean Startup*, Eric Ries
- *Product-Led Growth*, Wes Bush
- *Scientific Advertising*, Claude C. Hopkins
- *The Elements of User Onboarding*, Samuel Hulick
- *This Won't Scale*, Drift

Glossary

Activation rate: The percentage of users who achieve success with the product.

Aha Moment: The moment when users first perceive the product as valuable.

ARPU (Average Revenue per User): The average revenue generated per user per month.

ARPPU (Average Revenue per Paying User): The average revenue generated per customer per month.

ARR (Annual Recurring Revenue): The value of recurring revenue of a business's term subscriptions normalized to a single calendar year.

Behavioral emails: Automated emails sent to recipients based on their actions and behavior. Sometimes also known as lifecycle emails.

Burn Rate: How quickly your cash holdings are decreasing, typically expressed on a per month basis.

B2B (Business to Business): Companies who sell products chiefly to other businesses, rather than selling them to consumers.

B2C (Business to Consumer): Companies who sell products directly to consumers.

Click rate: The ratio of how many people open your email to how many people click on it.

Cohorts: A group of users that are grouped together based on a common attribute, for example the month they signed up, the source through which you acquired them, etc.

Cold email: An unsolicited email that is sent to a receiver without prior contact. It's the email equivalent to a cold call.

Conversion: Every time a user moves forward a step in your funnel from visitor (just visiting your website) to user (signed up) to customer (paying you money) to referrer (helping bring you new users).

Churn: The number of customers or subscribers who stop using your service during a given time period.

CLV (Customer Lifetime Value): The predicted amount a customer will spend on your product or service throughout the entire relationship.

CTA (Call-to-Action): The one thing you want people to click on your page or in your email.

Customer journey: A series of all touchpoints a customer has with a company, brand, and product to reach a certain milestone.

Delivery rate: The percentage of emails that were actually delivered to recipients' inboxes, calculated by subtracting hard and soft bounces from the gross number of emails sent, then dividing that number by gross emails sent.

Desired outcome: What the customer needs to achieve irrespective of your product and how they need to achieve it.

Email subscriber: A prospect, user, or customer who permits a particular brand to send them emails.

Expansion revenue: When paying customers increase their subscription amount.

Freemium: A customer acquisition strategy that provides access to part of a software product to prospects free of charge, without a time limit.

Free trial: A customer acquisition strategy that provides a partial or complete product to prospects free of charge for a limited time.

KPI (Key Performance Indicator): A metric that demonstrates how effectively a company is achieving its key business objectives.

Landing page: A specific page distinct from your main website that has one goal and one call-to-action.

Lifecycle emails: Automated emails sent to recipients based on their actions and behavior.

Marketing automation: Using software to automate marketing activities.

MPA (Minimum Path to Awesome): The optimal path to value discovery in your product.

MRR (Monthly Recurring Revenue): The amount of monthly subscription revenue generated by your customers.

MVP (Minimum Viable Product): The version of a new product which allows a team to collect the maximum amount of learning about customers with the least effort.

Nurturing: The process of nurturing relationships with potential customers at every stage of the sales funnel.

NPS (Net Promoter Score): A survey methodology used to evaluate customer satisfaction and loyalty.

Onboarding: The process that new customers go through when they are becoming customers.

Open rate: The percentage of people who open your email. The open rate is calculated by dividing the number of emails opened by the total number of emails sent, excluding bounced messages.

QA (Quality Assurance): A way of preventing mistakes and defects in products and avoiding problems when delivering products to customers.

Reactivation: The act of winning back churned or disengaged users or customers.

Referral rate: The percentage of current users who refer new users.

Retention: Any usage after the initial use. Retention is the most important aspect of a successful SaaS business.

Revenue churn: Churn measured by the dollar amount of contracts lost.

ROI (Return on Investment): A performance measure used to evaluate the efficiency of an investment or compare the efficiency of a number of different investments.

Runway: The number of months of cash the company has to operate at the current burn rate.

SaaS (Software as a Service): A software licensing and delivery model in which software is licensed on a subscription basis.

TTV (Time to Value): The amount of time it takes a new customer to realize value from a product.

Unit economics: The direct revenues and associated costs, expressed on a per user basis.

User acquisition: A new user sign up. This may be either a new user on a free trial, or a permanently free version.

Value metric: The metric that best correlates with what your customers perceive as valuable in your product.

Notes

WHY EMAIL MARKETING STILL MATTERS TODAY

1   https://litmus.com/blog/infographic-the-roi-of-email-marketing

2   https://coherentpath.com/rarelogic/blog/how-does-email-marketing-roi-compare-to-other-digital-channels

3   https://blog.hubspot.com/marketing/email-marketing-stats

4   https://www.useronboard.com/The-Elements-of-User-Onboarding-Intro.pdf

EMAIL MARKETING DOESN'T HAVE TO BE COMPLICATED

5   https://www.slideshare.net/dmc500hats/startup-metrics-for-pirates-long-version

UNDERSTANDING YOUR USERS AND CUSTOMERS

6   https://econsultancy.com/anti-personas-definition-benefits

DEFINING NECESSARY CUSTOM FIELDS

7   250 custom data attributes (including archived attributes) at the time of writing.

CREATING A DATA IMPLEMENTATION PLAN

8   https://segment.com/industry/startups

9   https://tagmanager.google.com

WHY SPEED MATTERS

10   https://themeforest.net

RESEARCHING EMAIL COPY & DESIGNS

11   https://reallygoodemails.com

12   https://www.goodemailcopy.com

13   https://goodsalesemails.com

14   https://www.mailcharts.com

15   https://mailody.io

EMAIL SEQUENCE PACING & STRUCTURE

16   https://meetedgar.com/blog/hacked-mailchimp-ab-test-automated-campaigns

EFFECTIVE EMAIL COPYWRITING

17 https://en.wikipedia.org/wiki/Fear_of_missing_out

18 https://en.wikipedia.org/wiki/AIDA_(marketing)

SUBJECT LINE COPYWRITING

19 https://snov.io/blog/550-spam-trigger-words-to-avoid-in-2019

20 https://www.campaignmonitor.com/blog/email-marketing/2019/05/email-marketing-in-the-era-of-8-second-attention-spans

21 https://www.gethighlights.co/blog/emojis-in-subject-lines

22 https://sendcheckit.com/email-subject-line-tester

23 https://www.gethighlights.co/blog/email-subject-line-tester-olympics

24 https://kopywritingkourse.com/subject-line-generator-formula

DO THIS BEFORE SETTING AN EMAIL LIVE

25 https://www.getyoursaasonboard.com/read/how-to-decide-which-emails-in-a-series-to-keep

SETTING UP REPORTING

26 https://web.archive.org/web/20060207175958/http://www.mailchimp.com/screenshots/screen3.phtml

27 https://litmus.com/blog/infographic-the-2019-email-client-market-share

28 https://www.gethighlights.co

TRACKING LIST HYGIENE

29 https://www.senderscore.org

30 https://litmus.com/spam-filter-tests

31 https://www.emailonacid.com/spam-testing

32 https://documentation.mailjet.com/hc/en-us/articles/360043227913-What-is-a-good-unsubscribe-rate-

THE PROBLEM AND LIMITS OF BENCHMARKS

33 https://mailchimp.com/resources/email-marketing-benchmarks

TESTING USEFULNESS

34 https://ga-dev-tools.appspot.com/campaign-url-builder

35 https://www.gethighlights.co/blog/setup-google-analytics-saas-app

36 https://www.gethighlights.co/blog/setup-google-analytics-goals

OPTIMIZING EMAIL DELIVERABILITY

37 https://returnpath.com/wp-content/uploads/2015/10/2015-Deliverability-Benchmark-Report.pdf

38 https://www.senderscore.org

39 https://www.senderscore.org/blocklistlookup

40 https://spamcheck.postmarkapp.com

41 https://www.mail-tester.com

42 https://litmus.com/spam-filter-tests

43 https://www.emailonacid.com/spam-testing

44 https://snov.io/blog/550-spam-trigger-words-to-avoid-in-2019

OPTIMIZING EMAIL OPENS

45 https://blog.hubspot.com/sales/sales-email-subject-never-try

46 https://sendcheckit.com/email-subject-line-tester

47 https://www.subjectline.com

48 https://coschedule.com/email-subject-line-tester

49 https://www.gethighlights.co/blog/email-subject-line-tester-olympics

OPTIMIZING EMAIL BODY (OFFER, ETC)

50 http://www.hemingwayapp.com

51 https://www.boomeranggmail.com

52 https://www.htmlemailcheck.com

53 https://litmus.com

54 https://putsmail.com

55 https://www.emailonacid.com

56 https://www.youtube.com/watch?v=SOtdJl4PKf8&feature=youtu.be&t=18m22s

57 https://www.dictionary.com/e/acronyms/tldr

OPTIMIZING LANDING PAGES (PAGE GOAL, ETC)

58 https://developers.google.com/speed/pagespeed/insights

59 https://gs.statcounter.com/press/mobile-and-tablet-internet-usage-exceeds-desktop-for-first-time-worldwide

60 You can get a free SSL certificate via https://letsencrypt.org.

61 https://fivesecondtest.com

62 https://www.hotjar.com

63 https://www.crazyegg.com

64 https://readable.com

65 https://www.cxpartners.co.uk/our-thinking/web_forms_design_guidelines_an_eyetracking_study

COLD EMAIL SEQUENCES

66 https://blog.sellingpower.com/gg/2011/10/how-cold-calling-20-added-100-million-to-salesforcecoms-revenues.html

67 https://www.youtube.com/watch?v=mDnddmAxUNA

68 https://www.cnbc.com/2017/02/10/birchbox-ceo-sending-great-cold-emails-was-how-i-first-found-success.html

69 https://www.youtube.com/watch?v=nTUOILK2wyc

70 https://hunter.io

71 https://www.zoominfo.com

72 https://www.voilanorbert.com

73 https://connect.clearbit.com

74 https://www.yesware.com/blog/find-email-addresses

75 https://youtu.be/SOtdJl4PKf8?t=1088

76 https://mailshake.com

77 https://www.yesware.com

78 https://www.streak.com

79 https://www.youtube.com/watch?v=VOgSJqmyLEQ

80 https://reply.io/7-sales-blunders

81 https://woodpecker.co/blog/warm-prospects

82 https://www.drift.com/blog/inbound-automation-whiteboard-lessons

83 https://clearbit.com/reveal

84 https://www.leadfeeder.com

85 https://www.lemlist.com

86 https://www.loom.com

87 https://www.upwork.com

88 https://www.fiverr.com

WELCOME & ONBOARDING SEQUENCES

89 https://sixteenventures.com/customer-success-desired-outcome

90 https://growthhackers.com/questions/ask-gh-how-do-you-determine-which-tests-to-run-on-a-site-when-looking-to-optimize-conversion-rates

91 https://www.appcues.com/blog/pirate-metric-saas-growth

92 https://www.experian.com/assets/marketing-services/white-papers/welcome-email-report.pdf

93 https://virayo.com/saas/customer-onboarding

94 https://outfunnel.com/onboarding-automation

95 https://tomtunguz.com/top-10-learnings-from-the-redpoint-free-trial-survey

96 https://blog.madkudu.com/50-of-saas-conversions-happen-after-trial-ends

97 https://www.youtube.com/watch?v=tfQNJpnxmMw

98 https://blog.madkudu.com/50-of-saas-conversions-happen-after-trial-ends

99 https://blog.returnpath.com/best-practices-for-a-successful-onboarding-series

BEHAVIORAL & LIFECYCLE EMAILS

100 The funnel is based on the A.A.R.R. framework: https://www.slideshare.net/dmc500hats/startup-metrics-for-pirates-long-version

101 https://customer.io/blog/what-are-lifecycle-emails-patio11-patrick-mckenzie

UPGRADE, UPSELL & EXPANSION REVENUE SEQUENCES

102 https://www.process.st/freemium-conversion-rate

103 https://www.oreilly.com/library/view/marketing-metrics-the/9780134086040

104 https://en.wikipedia.org/wiki/Loss_aversion

105 https://www.profitwell.com/blog/nps-retention-benchmarks

106 https://www.priceintelligently.com/blog/saas-discounting-strategy-lowers-ltv-by-over-30-percent

RETENTION SEQUENCES

107 The direct revenues and associated costs, expressed on a per user basis.

108 https://www.forentrepreneurs.com/why-churn-is-critical-in-saas

109 https://www.youtube.com/watch?v=ch7aps2h8zQ

110 https://www.saasemailmarketing.net/articles/promote-annual-subscription-improve-retention-cashflow

111 https://www.priceintelligently.com/blog/profit-well-march-2018/the-profitwell-report-the-worlds-largest-study-on-churn-17

112 http://churnbuster.io

113 https://www.profitwell.com/churn-reduction-software

114 https://www.chargebee.com/blog/saas-business-growth-findings

115 https://vimeo.com/72140534

116 https://www.profitwell.com/blog/driving-higher-nps-benchmarks

117 https://www.intercom.com/resources/books/intercom-product-management

118 https://en.wikipedia.org/wiki/Unboxing

119 https://sixteenventures.com/saas-customer-success-zombie-customers

120 https://www.slideshare.net/seanellis/building-a-companywide-growth-culture-saastr-annual-2016/23-Final_Thought_Focus_on_Value

REFERRAL SEQUENCES

121 https://www.bloomberg.com/news/articles/2016-05-04/tasty-taco-helpful-hygienist-are-all-those-surveys-of-any-use

122 https://articles.uie.com/net-promoter-score-considered-harmful-and-what-ux-professionals-can-do-about-it

123 https://hbr.org/2003/12/the-one-number-you-need-to-grow

124 https://medium.com/airbnb-engineering/hacking-word-of-mouth-making-referrals-work-for-airbnb-46468e7790a6

125 https://www.nielsen.com/us/en/insights/article/2012/consumer-trust-in-online-social-and-mobile-advertising-grows

126 https://www.wootric.com

127 https://delighted.com

128 https://www.promoter.io

129 https://www.asknicely.com

130 https://survicate.com

131 http://www.npscalculator.com

132 https://blog.upscope.io/health-score

133 https://medium.com/@audreymelnik/how-to-automate-your-nps-survey-4ad95ba8cd5

REACTIVATION SEQUENCES

134 https://www.youtube.com/watch?v=tfQNJpnxmMw

135 https://www.productled.org/data-and-trends/state-of-product-led-growth

136 https://neilpatel.com/blog/re-engage-dead-email-subscribers

137 https://mailchimp.com/resources/inactive-subscribers-are-still-valuable-customers

138 https://www.businessofapps.com/marketplace/push-notifications/research/push-notifications-statistics

139 https://www.getvero.com/resources/making-the-most-of-your-funnel-the-hail-mary-email

About the Author

Étienne is a three-time startup founder (Flagback, HireVoice, and Highlights) and the author of Solving Product, Lean B2B, and Find Your Market. The Lean B2B methodology helps thousands of entrepreneurs and innovators around the world build successful businesses.

In 2015, Étienne joined LANDR as head of customer engagement. There, he helped create and optimize a full customer lifecycle communication program that contributed to a revenue growth of 4x in two years.

You can connect with me on:
- https://saasplaybook.co
- https://twitter.com/egarbugli
- https://www.linkedin.com/in/egarbugli

Subscribe to my newsletter:
- https://saasplaybook.co/newsletter

Also by Étienne Garbugli

Étienne's books focus on leveraging customer insights to build and grow businesses.

Solving Product

https://solvingproduct.com/pdf

Solving Product offers a simple, unique, and wildly powerful business compass.

It was carefully designed to help product teams and entrepreneurs reveal the gaps in their business models, find new avenues for growth, and systematically overcome their next hurdles by leveraging the greatest resource at their disposal—their customers.

Lean B2B: Build Products Businesses Want

https://leanb2b.co/pdf

Lean B2B consolidates the best thinking around Business-to-Business (B2B) customer development to help technology entrepreneurs quickly find traction in the enterprise, leaving as little as possible to luck.

The Lean B2B methodology is used by thousands of entrepreneurs and innovators around the world.

Printed in the USA
CPSIA information can be obtained
at www.ICGtesting.com
LVHW011339061223
765524LV00096B/3688